D0909184

The toils of scepticism

The Toils of Scepticism

JONATHAN BARNES

*Professor of Ancient Philosophy in the University of Oxford,
and Fellow of Balliol College*

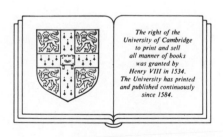

The right of the
University of Cambridge
to print and sell
all manner of books
was granted by
Henry VIII in 1534.
The University has printed
and published continuously
since 1584.

CAMBRIDGE UNIVERSITY PRESS

Cambridge

New York   Port Chester

Melbourne   Sydney

Published by the Press Syndicate of the University of Cambridge
The Pitt Building, Trumpington Street, Cambridge CB2 1RP
40 West 20th Street, New York, NY 10011, USA
10 Stamford Road, Oakleigh, Melbourne 3166, Australia

First published 1990

Printed in Great Britain at the University Press, Cambridge

British Library cataloguing in publication data

Barnes, Jonathan, 1942–
The toils of scepticism.
1. Greek philosophy, ancient period. Scepticism
I. Title
186
ISBN 0-521-38339-0

Library of Congress cataloguing in publication data

Barnes, Jonathan.
The toils of scepticism/Jonathan Barnes.
p.   cm.
ISBN 0-521-38339-0
1. Sextus, Empiricus. 2. Skepticism–History. I. Title.
B623.B37   1990
186′.1–dc20   89-27951 CIP

ISBN 0 521 38339 0 hardback

SE

Contents

Introduction

Greek philosophy knew two main varieties of scepticism, one taking its name from Pyrrho of Elis and the other associated with a particular phase in the history of Plato's Academy. My concern in this book is with Pyrrhonian scepticism, and I say nothing about the Academic variety. For the sake of brevity, I usually leave the words 'sceptic' and 'scepticism' without a qualifying adjective; it should be understood that it is the Pyrrhonian sceptic and Pyrrhonian scepticism to which I mean to refer.

Pyrrhonian scepticism had a long career, in the course of which it assumed significantly different forms. For us, its chief representative is Sextus Empiricus, the only Pyrrhonian whose works have survived. I shall be concerned, almost exclusively, with the scepticism which is expressed in the pages of Sextus. Thus I ignore the earlier phases of Pyrrhonism, which pose special problems both of an historical and of a philosophical nature;[1] and I ignore the few texts outside Sextus which offer us additional evidence for the later history of the Pyrrhonian philosophy.

Of Sextus himself we know little.[2] He was a doctor by profession. He lived in the second century AD. He was a prolific author, but not an original thinker. We possess three of his writings. One offers an outline of scepticism, giving first a general account of the nature of Pyrrhonism and then a survey of the arguments which the Pyrrhonians advanced against the Dogmatists. ('The Dogmatists', οἱ δογματικοί, is the title by which the sceptics referred generically

---

1 For Pyrrho himself (c.360–270 BC) see the fundamental study by Fernanda Decleva Caizzi, *Pirrone – testimonianze* (Naples, 1981).
2 See, most recently, D.K. House, 'The Life of Sextus Empiricus', *Classical Quarterly* 30, 1980, 227–38.

to non-sceptical philosophers.) The destructive arguments are arranged in three sections, corresponding to the three traditional parts of Dogmatic philosophy, logic and physics and ethics. A second work collects a larger quantity of these destructive arguments, similarly organized in three sections. A third work consists of six essays directed against six Dogmatic arts – grammar, rhetoric, geometry, arithmetic, astrology, music.[3] In all three of his works Sextus is largely concerned to assemble and arrange existing material: he draws on – and, sometimes at least, actually copies from – earlier Pyrrhonian sources.[4]

It is a difficult question whether the three works present a single and coherent form of Pyrrhonism. Some scholars find important differences among the works, and some scholars find important differences within the works – differences which are perhaps to be explained by the interesting hypothesis that Sextus' own views underwent some change or development, or else by the dispiriting hypothesis that Sextus nonchalantly drew on different sources in different parts of his writings. Such suppositions and hypotheses raise issues of scholarly significance, but in this book I pass them by.

My particular subject is what I may call the Agrippan aspect of Sextus' scepticism, the aspect which in some fashion derives from the shadowy figure of Agrippa.[5] Much of Sextus' work is Agrippan in inspiration or colouring, but by no means all of his thought was moulded by Agrippa. (And so I shall say nothing about some of the most celebrated parts of Sextus' writings which derive from the

---

3 The three works are: (1) *Outlines of Pyrrhonism*, in three Books (the title is customarily abbreviated to *PH*); (2) a work in five Books, normally known as *Against the Mathematicians* VII–XI (the title is abbreviated to *M*); and (3) the six Books of *Against the Mathematicians* I–VI (also abbreviated to *M*). As the titles indicate, *M* VII–XI and *M* I–VI used to be printed as parts of a single treatise, but they are two perfectly distinct works, and the modern nomenclature is unfortunate.

4 For Sextus as a copyist see Jonathan Barnes, 'Diogene Laerzio e il Pirronismo', *Elenchos* 7, 1986, 385–427, with references to the pioneering studies by Karel Janáček. (Add now K. Janáček, "Ο ἐξ ὑποθέσεως τρόπος', *Eirene* 24, 1987, 55–65.)

5 Agrippa is referred to by Diogenes Laertius (IX 88); and he is presumably the eponym of the *Agrippa*, written by an unknown sceptic called Apellas (see Diogenes Laertius, IX 106). Otherwise he is never mentioned in the ancient texts. We may reasonably conjecture that he flourished at the end of the first century BC (see below, pp.121–2), and hence a century and a half before Sextus.

somewhat less obscure figure of Aenesidemus.[6]) Again, my interest focusses on a single facet of the Agrippan aspect of Sextus' Pyrrhonism. For it is the general form which Agrippan argumentation characteristically takes and the general structures which Agrippan scepticism characteristically erects which constitute the central theme of this book. And I pay little attention, except by way of occasional illustration, to the numerous particular instances of these forms and structures which occur throughout Sextus' writings.

After such disclaimers, the reader may pardonably wonder if he has not opened a book of piddling breadth, a learned monograph – or, at least, a monograph – which prescinds from everything which made ancient scepticism a subtle and living philosophy, and which limits its outlook by the close and narrowing blinkers of leathery scholarship.

But I claim three things for my circumscribed subject. First, and exegetically: that the forms and structures I discuss were among the most important aspects of Pyrrhonism, so that to study them is to study the soul of ancient scepticism. Secondly, and historically: that these same forms and structures have had a unique influence on the subsequent history of sceptical enquiry, and hence, more generally, on the history of epistemology or the enquiry into the nature and scope of human knowledge: the Agrippan forms lie at the heart of the western philosophical tradition. Thirdly, and philosophically: that these forms and structures remain today among the central issues in the theory of knowledge; that every modern epistemologist must take notice of them; and that they still provide the subject of epistemology with some of its most cunning puzzles and most obdurate problems.

My book has both exegetical and philosophical pretensions. Exegetically, it centres, as I have said, on Sextus. I have attempted to give a comprehensive treatment of my topics insofar as they appear in Sextus' pages. In addition, I have from time to time referred to other ancient authors and ancient texts. Here I have not, of course, been exhaustive in my citations or references; rather, I

---

6 Aenesidemus flourished in the first half of the first century BC. But little enough is reported about him – and most of that is controversial. See e.g. John Glucker, *Antiochus and the Late Academy* (Göttingen, 1978), pp.116–19.

have picked a small sample of texts in order to indicate that Sextus and the Pyrrhonists were, from an intellectual point of view, neither hermits nor pariahs – their concerns and interests concerned and interested other philosophers and scientists.

The book is not an introduction to ancient Pyrrhonism.[7] But I have tried to make my historical remarks elementary and I have tried to avoid esoteric scholarship. I hope that readers with no antecedent knowledge of Greek philosophy will find the book intelligible. Historical allusions in the text call upon no pre-existing acquaintance. (And the Note on the ancient authors offers a minimal *mise en scène*.) All quotations from ancient works are done into English; and those few Greek words which appear in the body of the book are all explained on their first appearance. (The footnotes sometimes cite Greek without translation.) Greek words are written in the Greek alphabet. I was once a champion of transliteration, but I now find it both aesthetically displeasing and pedagogically fatuous – I cannot believe that an intelligent and Greekless reader who has had the Greek term for disagreement Englished for him will somehow find it easier to understand the sign '*diaphônia*' than the sign 'διαφωνία'.

The philosophical pretensions of the book are modest. All the issues I discuss arise from the work of Sextus. I have, of course, selected those points which I – and, I hope, other philosophers – find exciting; and I have on occasion developed a point somewhat further than the Greek texts do. But my ambitions are essentially determined by the texts. I have been concerned primarily to describe and present the real philosophical difficulties which the texts raise. I do not claim to have resolved any of the difficulties. I do not even claim to have contributed to their resolution – except insofar as a plain description may itself make such a contribution.

I hope that the philosophical parts of the book will be intelligible to readers who may be interested in ancient thought but have no antecedent knowledge of modern philosophy. I have tried to avoid jargon, and I have tried to avoid covert allusions to modern issues or modern authors. I have also tried to write plainly and to write with lucidity. But the issues are difficult – or so I find – and I am sure that I have left some things vexatiously dark and obscure. I have

---

7 For that I may refer to Julia Annas and Jonathan Barnes, *The Modes of Scepticism* (Cambridge, 1985).

sometimes set out arguments in a modestly formal manner. In a very few places I have used a few of the logical symbols which pepper modern philosophical writings. I do not see why symbols, once explained, should deter. But numerous readers are allegedly unsettled by them, and whenever I have used them I have also given a paraphrase in ordinary language.

The five chapters of the book derive from five lectures which I gave in Naples in April 1988. The written text does not present exactly what I said; but it remains the text of a set of lectures, and it retains some of the looseness and informality which lecturers are customarily allowed.

I have added a few footnotes. (Many of them are simply lists of references, which look ugly if set out in the text.) It is easy enough to clog the bottom of a page with annotations; but more often than not such stuff rather displays the author's learning than forwards the reader's understanding. At any rate, that is my current excuse for idleness.

Again, the book contains no bibliography and few bibliographical references. There are several excellent bibliographies of Pyrrhonism in print,[8] and there is no need to publish another. As for references, I have used them for one purpose only, viz. to direct the reader to discussions of matters which are not dealt with in my own text. (Even here I have been selective, and in particular, I have not thought it appropriate to give running references to the vast modern literature in the theory of knowledge.[9]) Lest this practice

8 There is an introductory bibliography on Pyrrhonism in Annas and Barnes, op. cit. n.7; and a full one by Luciana Ferraria and Giuseppina Santese, in Gabriele Giannantoni (ed.), *Lo scetticismo antico* (Naples, 1981). For an excellent bibliographical introduction to Hellenistic philosophy in general see volume 2 of A.A. Long and D.N. Sedley, *The Hellenistic Philosophers* (Cambridge, 1987). The bibliographical record published each year in the journal *Elenchos* will keep the brazen-bowelled up to date.

9 Of the modern literature I think I have gained most from P.F. Strawson, *Skepticism and Naturalism – some Varieties* (London, 1985); Laurence BonJour, *The Structure of Empirical Knowledge* (Cambridge Mass, 1985); Alvin I. Goldman, *Epistemology and Cognition* (Cambridge Mass, 1986); John Pollock, *Contemporary Theories of Knowledge* (London, 1986); and from the articles collected by G.S. Pappas and Marshall Swain, *Essays on Knowledge and Justification* (Ithaca NY, 1978), and by Hilary Kornblith, *Naturalizing Epistemology* (Cambridge Mass, 1985). There is a helpful recent survey by Ernest Sosa, 'Beyond Scepticism, to the Best of our Knowledge', *Mind* 97, 1988, 153–88.

seem intolerably immodest, I should perhaps say – what will be evident to any professional who may chance upon this book – that I do indeed owe a very great deal to earlier philosophers and scholars. Like all other students of Pyrrhonism, I have, for example, learned much from Victor Brochard's *Les sceptiques grecs*. If I do not write 'cf. Brochard' at the foot of every fifth page, that does not mean that I am not indebted to Brochard at least so often.

The five lectures were given at the invitation of the Istituto Italiano per gli Studi Filosofici. I am deeply grateful to the President of the Institute, Avvocato Gerardo Marotta, and to its Director, Professor Giovanni Pugliese Carrattelli, for inviting me to speak on scepticism in the elegant and learned surroundings of the Palazzo Serra di Cassano. I am grateful, too, to the Secretary General of the Institute, Professor Antonio Gargano, for his generous and unobtrusive aid.

I thank my Naples audiences for the helpful comments and criticisms which they offered, and also for the courtesy and patience with which they suffered my vile Italian.

Earlier versions of some of the lectures were delivered as papers to various groups and gatherings: at the Universities of Göttingen, Oxford, Zürich, Bern, York, Alberta, Princeton, Budapest and Pecs, and at the London School of Economics. On each of these occasions I suspect that I learned more from my audience than they learned from me.

The final typescript was scrutinized by two referees for the Cambridge University Press. Their anonymous remarks enabled me to make a number of substantial improvements to the text.

Over the years I have accumulated more debts to friends and colleagues than I can readily recall. Several of the ideas which I here put forward as my own were certainly suggested, implicitly or explicitly, by others. I hope that the true begetters will be content with a general expression of gratitude – and more flattered than vexed if I have ploughed with their heifers. I cannot name them all individually, and to select some would be invidious.

Sextus once had the status of an influential thinker, and he was once read as an important philosopher. I do not think that he was a great philosopher, of the rank of an Aristotle or a Chrysippus or a

Galen. But I do think that his works contain a quantity of good philosophy. His reputation is now once more on the rise. If this book helps to persuade one or two readers to look seriously at Sextus and at ancient Pyrrhonism, it will have achieved all it can decently hope for.

Oxford   JONATHAN BARNES
June 1989

Disagreement

In a dialogue written by the satirist Lucian, Menippus relates how he determined to abandon all worldly pursuits – wealth and office and power – and resolved to study science and the nature of things. At first he was overwhelmed by doubt and perplexity. In order to defeat the doubt and disentangle the perplexity, he sought out the best philosophers and scientists of the age – and he paid vast sums for his tuition. The fees, he complained, were wasted.

> So far from releasing me from my original ignorance, they actually plunged me into greater perplexities, drowning me every day with principles and ends and atoms and voids and matters and ideas and the like. And what seemed hardest of all to me was that, although no one of them said the same thing as any other but all uttered conflicting and contrary statements, yet each thought to persuade me and tried to convert me to his own view.

To which Menippus' companion ironically replies:

> How extraordinary that these wise men should fight with one another over the facts and not hold the same opinions on the same matters. *(Icaromenippus 5)*

Faction and disagreement, conflict and dispute, were endemic among scientists and philosophers in the second century AD. *Plus ça change.*

Galen, Lucian's contemporary and the leading medical scientist of his age, was impressed and troubled by the disagreement he found among his fellow-scientists. He refers repeatedly to the disputes which exercised the doctors. His own technical writings often start by rehearsing a dispute, which they then attempt to resolve.[1] He composed separate essays about disagreements and about ways of solving disagreements.[2]

Disagreement – or διαφωνία, to use the commonest of several Greeks words for the phenomenon – was a normal feature of the medical world of Galen's day; indeed, it was an institutionalized feature. For medical men would usually belong to a sect or school (a αἵρεσις, whence the English 'heresy'); and the sects were distinguished one from another precisely by their doctrinal differences. Nor was that all: even within a sect there was likely to be internecine strife, and whatever school you subscribed to – whether you were a Pneumatic or an Erasistratean or a Herophilean or a Methodic – you would find enemies at home as well as abroad.[3]

If disagreement was normal among the scientists, it was notorious among the philosophers. And it was notorious a century before Galen complained. Philosophical διαφωνία was a commonplace in Seneca's day, and allowed him a little joke: *facilius inter philosophos quam inter horologia conveniet* – You're more likely to find two philosophers in agreement than two clocks (*apocol* II 2). Earlier still, this outrageous *dissensio* had encouraged a Roman proconsul who was passing through Athens to summon the disputing philosophers to a conference at which, whether ingenuously or disingenuously, he offered to arbitrate among their views and bring the scandal of philosophy to an end.[4]

As with the doctors, so with the philosophers, disagreement was institutionally enshrined. Most philosophers thought of themselves as belonging to a school or sect.[5] The main schools, Stoics and Epicureans, Peripatetics and Academics, defined themselves by their doctrines. And their doctrines, of course, conflicted.

1 See e.g. *nat fac* II 93 K; *us part* III 17 K; *PHP* V 288 K; *alim fac* VI 454 K; *syn puls* IX 443 K.

2 See e.g. *lib prop* XIX 38 K (*On the Disagreement among the Empirics*, three Books; *Against the Objections to 'On the Disagreement among the Empirics' and the Summaries of Theodas*, three essays); 45 K (*On Judging between those who Disagree in their Doctrines*); *ord lib prop* XIX 55 K (*On Disagreement in Anatomy*). These works have not survived.

3 See e.g. *meth med* X 35, 53, 125 K, on disagreements among the Methodics; Soranus, *gyn* III 2.

4 The man was L. Gellius Poplicola, the date 93 BC: see Cicero, *leg* I XX 53.

5 See D.N. Sedley, 'Philosophical Allegiance in the Greco-Roman World', in Miriam Griffin and Jonathan Barnes (edd.), *Philosophia Togata* (Oxford, 1989).

Again, there was disagreement within the schools. That the Stoics disagreed with one another was a commonplace. As for the Academics, Numenius wrote a petulant essay on their dissensions (Eusebius, *PE* xiv iv 16). Even the Epicureans, who were traditionally regarded as uncommonly harmonious and uniform in their views, indulged in domestic strife. The writings of Philodemus, preserved on the Herculaneum papyri, record several squabbles. Some members of the school, for example,

> refuse to say that sophistical rhetoric is an art of other things, as it in fact is, and want to prove that it is an art of the useless, and on each point they disagree (διαφωνοῦντες) with the Masters.   (*rhet* [PHerc 1674] xxix 13–21; cf. lii 19–21)

These renegades, as Philodemus characterizes them, were in their own eyes orthodox followers of the Masters of the Epicurean school.

Some philosophical disputes were no doubt trifling and terminological (or so Galen insists); but many were substantial and significant. Deep disagreement was a philosophical fact.

But if disagreement was a fact, what – if anything – did the fact imply? What attitude should a philosopher take to the disputes which certainly separated his school from other schools and which probably divided his own school within itself?

One attitude or reaction to dispute was an industrious resolve. Disagreement could be seen as a challenge and a spur. If you and I disagree we cannot both be right, so let us strive to determine who (if either of us) actually has truth on his side. In this way διαφωνία may stimulate philosophical research. A familiar aspect of Aristotle's philosophical procedure involves the collection of 'reputable opinions (ἔνδοξα)': these opinions will normally conflict with one another; but analysis and critical revision will eventually reveal the truths behind the disagreement and provide for the establishment of undisputed doctrine. And thus διαφωνία leads to knowledge.[6]

6 See e.g. Jonathan Barnes, 'Aristotle and the Methods of Ethics', *Revue Internationale de Philosophie* 133/134, 1980, 490–511. (For a later Peripatetic example see Jaap Mansfeld, '*Diaphonia*: the Argument of Alexander *De Fato* Chs. 1–2', *Phronesis* 33, 1988, 181–207.)

Galen, too, construed disagreement as a challenge – a challenge to uncover some reliable scientific and philosophical method.

> Drowning in the sea of disagreement among doctors, I turned to judge the matter, and recognized that I must first train myself in the methods of proof. This I did for many years.
> (*meth med* x 469 K)

Logic, for Galen, is the key to method (cf. *subf emp* 62.2–6 B), and it must be backed by arduous training. There is reason to think that it will succeed.

> Do not be downcast by the mass of disputing doctors and philosophers. If they all possessed the wherewithal to learn the truth and yet did not discover it, then it would indeed be reasonable for us to renounce any hope of discovery. But some of the prerequisites they do not possess (as they themselves actually admit), and in the case of others it is unclear whether they possess them or not. As for us, if we are aware that we possess all the wherewithal, then we may tackle the enquiry with confidence.   (*const art med* 1 243–4 K)

What are these prerequisites to discovery? They are seven: natural acumen; an early education in mathematics; submission to the best teachers of the age; indefatigable industry; a longing for the truth ('which very few have possessed'); a grasp of logical method; and constant practice in the method. 'If you possess all these things, what prevents you from enquiring into the truth with good hopes?' (*const art med* 1 244–5 K).

Galen thought that knowledge was attainable. He was an epistemological optimist. But his optimism was not inordinate.

> If we escape from the disagreements of the Dogmatists, we shall still be overcome on many matters; but on some issues we shall produce coherent theories, as the geometers and the arithmeticians do.   (*subf emp* 67.22–68.3 B)

And he was decidedly less sanguine about philosophy than about medicine. For

> in philosophical disagreements we have no sensory evidence – we cannot use sensory evidence to determine if the world is generated and destroyed, if there is void beyond it, if it is

infinite . . . And so with many other philosophical enquiries too – some disputes we cannot decide at all, and others require much research. But when it comes to what helps or harms the sick, matters are different; yet even so discovery still requires much time – and men of exceptional talent.

(*in Hipp morb acut* xv 434–5 K; cf. *PHP* v 766 K)

But if Galen thought that philosophical disagreements were harder to resolve than medical disagreements, he was not wholly pessimistic even on the philosophical front; and he certainly did not hold that the existence of disagreement was in itself a sign that the discovery of truth is beyond us. On the contrary, he supposed, in Aristotelian fashion, that disagreement should be a spur to industry, that διαφωνία should be an incentive to φιλοπονία.

Not everyone agreed with Galen. There was – not unexpectedly – disagreement about the proper attitude to disagreement. Thus Galen believed that we could discover the composition of the nonorganic parts of the body. But

we see the philosophers who embark on these enquiries – and some doctors too – differing widely among themselves. That, I think, is why most doctors seem to have given up such enquiries, supposing that what they are investigating cannot be discovered – and some have abandoned them on the grounds that they are not only impossible but also useless.

(*const art med* I 243 K)

The doctors who abandoned such enquiries were the Empirics, members of the medical school which denounced all theorizing and rejected any investigation into things imperceptible, and which maintained that medical science required nothing but perception and the collation of perceptions.[7] For the Empirics observed that

from the same phenomena different people infer different conclusions. And here they lay hold of the undecided disagreement (ἀνεπίκριτος διαφωνία) which they say is a sign of unknowability . . . Unknowability, they say, is a cause of undecided disagreement, and conversely disagreement is a sign of unknowability. It is disagreement about unclear

7 On the Empirics see e.g. the introduction to Michael Frede, *Galen: Three Treatises on the Nature of Science* (Indianapolis, 1985).

things, not about the phenomena, which is undecided. For with the phenomena, each thing appears as it is and bears witness to those whose views are true, refuting those whose views are false.   (*sect ingred* 1 78–9 K)

The same report can be read, a century before Galen, in the medical writer Celsus.

Those who are called Empirics . . . claim that enquiry into hidden causes and natural activities is pointless, since nature is not knowable. That it cannot be known is plain from the disagreements among those who have disputed over it – for on these points there is agreement neither among philosophers nor among the doctors themselves.

                              (*med* proem 27–8)

Thus the Empirics in effect regarded διαφωνία as a sort of disease, and (rather against their own theoretical position) they proposed an explanation or aetiology for it. If there is undecided disagreement, then that is a sign of unknowability: if there is undecided disagreement over some question (over the eternity of the universe, or the composition of the blood, or the physiological location of psychological functions), then we cannot possibly know the answer to the question. The disagreement thus points to the unknowability. And the unknowability in turn is the cause of the disagreement. That is the aetiology of the disease. And the therapy? Ignore the thing: if you can't know the answer to a question, then don't bother to ask it. The disagreement will not disappear but it will cease to irritate you.

A similar reaction to philosophical διαφωνία is found in a writer of a different profession and character. The disagreement of the pagan philosophers is a theme which runs through Eusebius' *Preparation for the Gospel*. Early in the work, Eusebius draws attention to 'their opposition to one another – for they agree in nothing and have filled everything with conflict and disagreement' (*PE* I viii 14); and at the end of Book xv he closes with tart references to 'their massive disagreement', to 'their rivalry with one another and their conflicts and their dissensions' (xv lxii 13, 15). The disagreement or διαφωνία among the Greeks and their philosophies contrasts with the agreement or συμφωνία of the Hebrews and their scriptures (e.g. xiv ii 1 ≈ iii 1). The moral is plain.

> Since the pagans themselves stood in diametrical opposition
> to one another and kindled useless conflicts and wars against
> themselves, surely absolutely anyone would reasonably al-
> low that for us suspension of judgement (ἐποχή) about these
> matters is the prudent course. (xv xxxii 9)

The medical Empirics were sceptics in matters hidden to perception. Eusebius urges ἐποχή or suspension of judgement in matters
philosophical. In each case, disagreement has generated a sceptical
conclusion.

Eusebius was not a philosophical sceptic; nor were the Empirics
philosophers by profession (though there were interesting links,
both theoretical and historical, between medical Empiricism and
philosophical scepticism). But both the Christian bishop and the
pagan quacks were prepared to infer a sceptical conclusion from
the διαφωνίαι they observed. Now the inference from διαφωνία to
scepticism was held to be especially characteristic of the
Pyrrhonian philosophers. In the following passage, Galen ad-
dresses Julianus, a Methodic doctor who claimed to be Stoic in
philosophical matters but who professed scepticism about the
chemical composition of bodies. Galen asks:

> Why should we not have precise knowledge of this, so long as
> we can provide a proof of the thesis and so long as the best
> philosophers – whom you yourself admire – agree with
> Hippocrates and with one another? Unless, of course, you
> think that the disagreement (διαφωνία) is sufficient evidence
> of our ignorance of the thesis, thus suddenly becoming a
> sceptic (ἀπορητικός) instead of a Stoic. For then you accept a
> theory which says that nothing which is a subject of disagree-
> ment among all the philosophers can possibly be available for
> human knowledge. (*adv Iul* xviiiA 268 K)

If Julianus bases his confession of ignorance on the fact of
διαφωνία, then he shows himself a sceptic. (The word ἀπορητικός
is a standard denomination of the Pyrrhonian sceptic: Sextus, *PH*
I 7.) For the idea that disagreement is a sign of ignorance and a
reason for suspension of judgement, is, according to Galen, the
characteristic mark of Pyrrhonian scepticism.

And Galen is right. Διαφωνίαι are referred to on countless

occasions[8] in the writings of Sextus Empiricus. For Sextus, disagreement is a fount and origin of scepticism, and this use and understanding of disagreement is utterly characteristic of Pyrrhonism. It is the Pyrrhonian use of διαφωνία which I want to discuss. If I have none the less begun this chapter by citing Galen and the Empirics and Eusebius, that is because I also want to insist that the argument from disagreement is not *peculiar* to Pyrrhonism. Some moderns regard the ancient sceptics as philosophical lightweights or dilettantes – as men whose arguments are profoundly superficial. Their outlandish views may amuse us, but they cannot enlighten us and they should not engage us. On one point at least – namely, the argument from disagreement – the Pyrrhonians developed a line of thought which commended itself to men of bottom: to sober doctors and to reverend bishops. Let us dare to treat Pyrrhonism seriously (which is no reason why it should not also be diverting).

The main question is this: What is the connexion between disagreement on the one hand and sceptical suspension of judgement on the other? What is the connexion between διαφωνία and ἐποχή? Before tackling the question, I had better say a little more about the two concepts which it links.

Ἐποχή was a term of art in ancient Pyrrhonism. Sextus explains it formally as follows:

8 '*Countless* occasions'? Well, I have counted about 120 uses of διαφωνία and its cognates; in addition, Sextus often uses στάσις or διάστασις and their cognates, or ἀμφισβήτησις and its cognates, or ἀνωμαλία and its cognates. There are occasional uses of μάχη and πόλεμος, and the like. Often the positive counterparts of διαφωνία (viz. συμφωνία, ὁμοφωνία, ὁμολογία etc.) indicate the presence of an argument from disagreement. (See Karel Janáček, *Sextus Empiricus' Sceptical Methods* (Prague, 1972), pp.73–80. Throughout this invaluable study, Janáček emphasizes Sextus' predilection for *variatio* in his choice of words. I suppose that in Sextus, and also in Galen (who is another lover of variety), the predilection is not *merely* stylistic: Sextus, like Galen, insists that it is fatuous to fuss over words – οὐ φωνομαχοῦμεν.) In all, there are more than 200 references, direct or oblique, to disagreement in Sextus' works; and there must be several hundred sections (i.e. numbered paragraphs in the modern editions) which are specifically concerned with using disagreement to sceptical ends. I have generally tried to give comprehensive documentation for my remarks about Sextus. Here I have been content with a sample set of references. Those who want more should turn to one of the most useful books yet written on ancient Pyrrhonism, viz. Karel Janáček, *Sexti Empirici Opera: IV Indices* (Leipzig, 1962²).

> Suspension of judgement is a standstill of the intellect, be-
> cause of which we neither reject nor accept anything.
> (*PH* I 10)

Thus:

> We take 'I suspend judgement' in the sense of 'I cannot say
> which of the offered views I should believe or disbelieve', thus
> showing that the matters seem equal to us with regard to
> warranty and lack of warranty.   (*PH* I 195)

In other words, I suspend judgement on, say, the immortality of the
soul if, having considered the matter, I neither reject nor accept the
soul's immortality, if I neither believe nor disbelieve that the soul is
immortal. (Why add the qualification 'having considered the matter'? Well, Sextus knew nothing about the fauna of South America.
He neither believed nor disbelieved that there are pangolins in
Patagonia. Did he then suspend judgement on the matter? No:
ἐποχή is something which comes about 'after the enquiry' (*PH* I 7),
and Sextus has not – could not have – made any investigation of the
fauna of the Americas.)

In schematic terms, I suspend judgement with regard to a proposition P if, having considered the matter, I neither believe that P nor
believe that not-P. More generally, I suspend judgement with
regard to the question ?Q if, having considered the matter, I neither
accept nor reject any answer to ?Q. My scepticism can be, of
course, more or less extensive. Every rational being is sceptical on
some issues ('When exactly was Sextus born?'). Some rational
beings are sceptical with regard to general areas of enquiry (as the
Empirics were sceptical about the underlying causes of diseases). In
the most extreme case, I might suspend judgement on every question I consider: I shall then have no considered beliefs or disbeliefs;
I shall be – as we may put it – a radical sceptic.

Ἐποχή is the heart of Pyrrhonian scepticism. It is clear that
Pyrrhonian scepticism is somewhat different from the scepticism
which Galen ascribes to the Empirical doctors. For the Empirics
hold that nothing can be known, they aver unknowability or
ἀκαταληψία. There is a difference between unknowability and
suspension of judgement. Since I am in a state of unknowability
with regard to ?Q if I hold that the answer to ?Q is not and cannot
be known, it is evident that I may suspend judgement over ?Q

9

without being in an attitude of ἀκαταληψία towards ?Q. For I may neither believe that ?Q is answerable nor believe that ?Q is not answerable. (I may – and, of course, a radical sceptic must – suspend judgement over the question of ἀκαταληψία.) Thus ἐποχή with regard to ?Q does not imply ἀκαταληψία with regard to ?Q. Nor, in the other direction, does ἀκαταληψία imply ἐποχή; for I may *believe* that P is the answer to ?Q while holding that no one can *know* the answer to ?Q. (Perhaps we cannot *know* whether Galen had read Sextus; but I myself believe that he had not.) Thus the difference between suspension and unknowability is clear in principle. Moreover, Sextus himself, whether rightly or wrongly,[9] distinguishes Pyrrhonian from Academic scepticism (and also from the philosophy of the Cyrenaics) precisely by the fact that Pyrrhonians stick with suspension while Academics (and also Cyrenaics) maintain unknowability (*PH* 1 1–3 and 215; cf. 226). Often, it is true, Sextus says – or seems to say – that Pyrrhonism embraces ἀκαταληψία.[10] These passages are admittedly puzzling. But most of them can, I think, be explained away (Sextus does not actually mean what he appears to say); and the rest may be put down to carelessness. However that may be, I shall speak as though Sextus consistently took suspension to be the sceptic's state of mind.

Thus the Pyrrhonists did not, officially, infer from διαφωνία to the particular sceptical conclusion which we have seen in the Empirics. Indeed, Sextus' official view is closer, in a way, to Galen's; for he insists that the sceptics continue to investigate (*PH* 1 3). The Greek word σκεπτικός, which I translate as 'sceptical', means literally 'enquiring'; and Sextus explains that

> the enquiring (σκεπτική) school of thought is also called investigative (ζητητική) from the activity of investigating and enquiring.　　　　　　　　　　　　　　　　　　　　(*PH* 1 7)

And he often remarks that the sceptic's ἐποχή holds good only 'up to now (μέχρι or ἀχρὶ νῦν)',[11] thereby hinting that future resolution of the doubt and future knowledge are not formally excluded.

9　On this see Gisela Stricker, 'Ueber den Unterschied zwischen den Pyrrhoneern und den Akademikern', *Phronesis* 26, 1981, 153–71.

10　See e.g. M 1 320: 'what is disagreed upon without decision is unknowable (ἀκατάληπτον)'; and cf. Janáček, *Methods*, pp.27–8.

11　See e.g. *PH* 1 25, 200, 201; III 70; M VII 380; VIII 118, 257, 401, 427/8; XI 229.

But we should not take this too seriously. Whatever Sextus may say, the Pyrrhonists did not – in any normal sense – prosecute philosophical and scientific researches; nor did they construe disagreement as a positive incentive and challenge in the Galenian spirit. None the less, it remains true that Pyrrhonian scepticism – Pyrrhonian ἐποχή – is, formally speaking, open-minded and in principle tolerant of future progress. Ἀκαταληψία is different: it locks the door to the temple of wisdom.

As for disagreement or διαφωνία, Sextus offers no official definition. It is, I suppose, worth saying first that διαφωνία is not mere *difference* of opinion. You and I may have different opinions without disagreeing on anything. Perhaps I believe that the toad is a mammal and you believe that it has magical properties. We are both wrong, but our opinions do not conflict. For disagreement to exist, there must be conflict: my opinion and your opinion must be incompatible or in conflict with one another.[12] Perhaps I hold that the toad is a mammal and you hold that it is an insect. (Note that if two opinions conflict, it does not follow that one of them must be correct. One, at least, must be wrong – and both *may* be wrong.)

Again, disagreement need not involve only two parties: if I take the toad to be a mammal and you take it to be an insect and the Zoologer Royal believes it to be a bird, then there is a διαφωνία *à trois*. Each of the three opinions is incompatible with each of the other two. Many of the disagreements Sextus chronicles are in fact of this multilateral sort: there were, after all, many different philosophers and several different philosophical schools, and each liked to disagree with all the others. But multilateral διαφωνίαι can always be analysed in terms of bilateral διαφωνίαι. We may say that x and y and z are in disagreement with one another if and only

12 What exactly is conflict here? It is more than 'non-compossibility'; that is to say, if two propositions cannot both hold together, it does not follow that they conflict with one another. For suppose that P is in itself impossible (let it be 'There is a highest prime number' or 'Sextus is both older and younger than Galen'); then P cannot hold together with any other proposition. For since P is impossible, the conjunction 'P and Q' is impossible for any proposition Q. But we should not want to say that P *conflicts* with every other proposition ('There is a highest prime number' does not conflict with 'Vesuvius is on the bay of Naples'). It is difficult to say precisely what conflict does consist in: it is, as it were, non-compossibility plus something else, but the something else is elusive. See e.g. M.R. Stopper, 'Schizzi Pirroniani', *Phronesis* 28, 1983, 265–97, at pp.285–6.

if x is in disagreement with y and y is in disagreement with z and x is in disagreement with z. (The account is easily generalized to cover any number of disputing parties.)

The parties to the disagreements which Sextus rehearses – the 'parts of the διαφωνία', as he often puts it[13] – are usually disputing philosophers; and the disagreements are usually disputes among the rival schools. (Sextus also notices some διαφωνίαι within the schools: e.g. *M* VII 228; VIII 400.) But disagreement is not, of course, limited by law to the professionals, and Sextus sometimes explicitly refers to disputes in ordinary life (βίος) or among laymen.[14]

Laymen, like professionals, are people; and in Sextus' writings the parties to a disagreement are usually persons or groups of people. Sometimes, however, Sextus will speak of a διαφωνία among the senses or among the phenomena or even among the 'things'.[15] If my sense of sight reports that a surface is smooth and my sense of touch reports that it is rough, then there is a disagreement between these two senses. If the Russian flag appears red to humans and grey to bulls, then there is a disagreement between these two appearances, between these two φαντασίαι. It is no doubt natural and intelligible to extend the concept of διαφωνία in this way; but the extension introduces new issues and new problems. In what follows I shall ignore this extended form of disagreement, which is not an essential part of Agrippan scepticism, and restrict my attention to διαφωνίαι among people.

Disagreements among the ancient philosophers often took the form of debates or disputes. Sextus, like Eusebius, uses political and military metaphors to describe the business. He speaks of factions and parties (στάσις and διάστασις), of wars and battles (πόλεμος and μάχη),[16] and he twice speaks in heightened terms of a πόλεμος ἄσπειστος, a war without truce.[17] These metaphors suggest actual debate, indeed heated dispute. But although disagreements may be manifested in debate and discussion, they need not

13 See *PH* I 50, 90, 98, 113; II 60, 67; III 182; *M* VII 318, 351; VIII 298.
14 See *PH* I 165, 185; III 65, 218, 233; *M* VIII 355; IX 60, 191; XI 43.
15 See e.g. *PH* II 52; *M* VII 345/6; VIII 182 (αἴσθησις); *PH* I 59, 112; *M* VII 177, 430 (φαντασία); *PH* I 12, 163; III 235 (πρᾶγμα).
16 For references see Janáček's *Indices*: more than 25 occurrences of factional words and about a dozen military terms.
17 See *PH* III 175; *M* XI 36 (where the MSS offer ἄπιστος and Fabricius emends to ἄσπειστος – though Mutschmann perversely determines to read ἄπιστος in both places).

be; for it is no part of the concept of διαφωνία that the parties to it be actively in dispute with one another. Indeed, there may be disagreement among the dead, who are certainly not still in debate and who in many cases did not even know of one another's existence. You and I are in disagreement about the taxonomy of the toad even if neither of us has heard of the other's foolish opinion. Disagreement is essentially a logical relation between our opinions and not a personal relation between us.

But disagreement is still a relation between *opinions*, between propositions held or opined. It is not simply a relation between propositions. The proposition that the toad is a mammal is not itself in disagreement with the proposition that the toad is an insect; it is the two *opinions* on the matter which show διαφωνία.

Thus we might think to define disagreement in roughly the following manner:

(D) x and y disagree (διαφωνοῦσι) over some issue ?Q, whenever x offers P_1 in answer to ?Q and y offers P_2 in answer to ?Q, and P_1 and P_2 are incompatible with one another.

So there is disagreement (διαφωνία) over a question ?Q if and only if at least two incompatible propositions have been offered in answer to it. For example,

there have been disagreements among the philosophers over the material elements. Pherecydes of Syrus said that earth was the first principle of everything; Thales of Miletus said water; Anaximander, his pupil, the infinite; Anaximenes and Diogenes of Apollonia, air . . . (*PH* III 30)

There is disagreement over the question: What are the material elements of the universe? For in answer to this question, Pherecydes gave one opinion (P_1), Thales another (P_2), Anaximander a third (P_3) and so on; and $P_1, P_2, P_3 \ldots$ are all mutually incompatible. Some of the parties to this multilateral dispute actually debated with one another. Most of them did not. But they were all in disagreement with one another.

This preliminary characterization of disagreement requires two further comments. First, suppose that you and I are discussing the authorship of the *Magna Moralia*, a treatise on ethics which is transmitted to us as part of the Aristotelian *corpus*. You hold that Aristotle wrote the *Magna Moralia*. I deny that he did, while offering no positive theory of my own. It is plain that there is a διαφωνία between us; and yet we might be reluctant to say that the two of us have given conflicting answers to the question 'Who wrote the *Magna Moralia*?', for we might be reluctant to say that I had answered the question at all.

The preliminary characterization of disagreement must be modified to account for cases of this sort. Of several possible modifications, I prefer the following: add a second clause to the definition of disagreement, and write it thus:

> (D1) x and y disagree over some issue ?Q whenever *either* x offers P₁ in answer to ?Q and y offers P₂ in answer to ?Q and P₁ and P₂ are incompatible, *or else* x offers P in answer to ?Q and y rejects P as an answer to ?Q (or *vice versa*).

This is a little cumbersome, but its import is plain: it amounts to no more than a pedantically precise way of saying that a διαφωνία is a conflict of opinion on some topic.

The second comment required by the preliminary characterization of disagreement is this. Sextus sometimes includes the sceptics themselves as parties to a disagreement – and the sceptics do not, of course, participate in a διαφωνία by virtue of holding an *opinion* on the issue, whatever it may be. I have in mind here not those several passages in which Sextus himself fictionally assumes the role of a non-sceptical thinker, producing opinions for the sake of argument and not *in propria persona*. Rather, I am thinking of those texts where ἐποχή is itself an option in the disagreement. For example, opening his account of the 'criterion of truth', Sextus says:

> Let us begin with the disagreement: of those who have discussed the criterion, some – e.g. the Stoics and others – have asserted that there is a criterion, others – including Xeniades of Corinth and Xenophanes of Colophon, who says
> > but belief is found over all –
> have claimed that there is not, and we suspend judgement as to whether there is or is not.　　　　　　　(*PH* II 17–18)

Is there a criterion of truth? Some say yes. Some say no. Some suspend judgement. There is disagreement, and it is trilateral. For the sceptics are themselves 'part' of the διαφωνία insofar as they suspend judgement on the matter.[18]

Neither (D) nor its successor, (D1), will accommodate this sort of διαφωνία. We need a further modification to the definition. Let us say that someone 'takes an attitude' to a question ?Q if, having considered the matter, he either *accepts* some proposition as the answer to ?Q or *rejects* some proposition as an answer to ?Q or *suspends judgement* over ?Q. Such attitudes may be said to conflict with one another in a variety of ways. Accepting P_1 will conflict with accepting P_2 when P_1 and P_2 are incompatible with one another. Rejecting P will conflict with accepting P. And suspending judgement over ?Q will conflict with any other attitude to ?Q. Then we may define disagreement simply enough, as follows:

(D2) x and y disagree over some issue ?Q whenever x and y hold conflicting attitudes to ?Q.

The successive characterizations of διαφωνία, (D), and (D1) and (D2), are related in the following way: anything which counts as a disagreement according to (D) also counts as a disagreement according to (D1), but not *vice versa*; anything which counts as a disagreement according to (D1) also counts as a disagreement according to (D2), but not *vice versa*. If we call the notions defined by (D), (D1) and (D2) respectively *positive* disagreement, disagreement *in opinion* and disagreement *in attitude*, then we may say that all positive disagreements are also disagreements in opinion, and all disagreements in opinion are also disagreements in attitude; but not the other way about.

Now although (D2) gives the largest – and, I suppose, the authoritative – explanation of what Sextus understands by a διαφωνία, as a matter of fact most of the disagreements which he reports are disagreements *in opinion*. My own discussion of διαφωνία will therefore usually be couched in terms of such disagreements. But we should remain aware of the possibility of disagreements in attitude which are not disagreements in opinion – and at one point in the discussion this possibility will have an interesting consequence.

18 See *PH* I 185; II 18, 31, 180, 259; III 23, 65, 119; *M* VIII 327, 334, 380; IX 60, 195; and cf. *M* I 28, where one Dogmatic party to a disagreement suspends judgement.

Well then, how does disagreement connect with suspension of judgement? How does διαφωνία lead to ἐποχή? Some passages in Sextus have suggested that disagreement is a *necessary* condition for suspension, in the sense that we cannot or shall not suspend judgement on an issue ?Q unless there is – or, perhaps, unless we are aware that there is – a διαφωνία over ?Q. And it is true that Sextus himself frequently introduces and describes a disagreement, sometimes at considerable length, before drawing any sceptical conclusion on a topic.[19] Now Sextus no doubt thinks that drawing attention to disagreement is a useful preliminary to other sceptical argumentation – it softens the reader up. But no text explicitly states, and none clearly implies, that disagreement is, in the strict sense, a necessary condition for suspension of judgement. Nor, of course, *should* Sextus have held that διαφωνία was an obligatory precondition for suspending judgement. For it would be absurd to imagine that I cannot suspend judgement on a topic unless at least two other people have held conflicting opinions on it; it would be absurd to suggest that I cannot be doubtful myself unless others have been sure – and sure in different directions. (I return briefly to this point in the final chapter.)

In any event, it is the converse relation which is the important one: Is διαφωνία a *sufficient* condition for ἐποχή? If there is a disagreement over ?Q, must we suspend judgement on the matter, neither accepting nor rejecting any proffered answer to the question?

At *PH* I 164–77 Sextus explains the five 'modes of suspension (τρόποι τῆς ἐποχῆς)' which 'the more recent sceptics hand down' (*PH* I 164). A 'mode' or τρόπος is, roughly speaking, an argument-form; and a mode of suspension is an argument-form which leads to suspension of judgement. The 'more recent' sceptics are identified for us by Diogenes Laertius, whose *Life* of Pyrrho contains an account of the Five Modes which closely parallels the account in Sextus (Diogenes, IX 88–9).[20] According to Diogenes, the Five Modes were presented by Agrippa (οἱ περὶ Ἄγριππαν). But since

---

19 See e.g. *PH* II 17; III 30; *M* VII 46, 261; VIII 3, 11. (These are passages where Sextus expressly remarks upon the fact that he is starting the sceptical discussion by setting out a διαφωνία.)

20 See Jonathan Barnes, 'Diogene Laerzio e il Pirronismo', *Elenchos* 7, 1986, 385–427.

we know next to nothing about Agrippa, the identification is not particularly informative.

The first of the Five Modes is called the mode 'from disagreement (ἀπὸ διαφωνίας)', and Sextus explains it as follows:

> The mode from disagreement is the one in virtue of which we discover that on any matter proposed there has been undecided faction (ἀνεπίκριτος στάσις) both among laymen (παρὰ τῷ βίῳ) and among the philosophers. And because of the dispute we cannot choose or reject anything, and so end in suspension of judgement. (*PH* I 165)

The mode of disagreement thus moves from στάσις, i.e. from διαφωνία, to ἐποχή. How and why does it do so?

A key term in the text is the adjective ἀνεπίκριτος. The verb ἐπικρίνειν, in the sense of 'decide' or 'determine' (a dispute), is ubiquitous in Sextus; and its standard use is precisely in connexion with disagreements – ἐπικρίνειν τὴν διαφωνίαν is to settle or decide the disagreement, to bring it to an end. Thus a disagreement is ἐπικριτός if there is a decision for it; and it is ἀνεπίκριτος (the adjective is formed with an 'alpha privative'), if there is no decision for it. But what is the precise force of the adjective? What exactly does it mean to say that 'there is no decision' for a dispute? There are two questions here. One, which I shall postpone, concerns the precise force of the verbal root ἐπικριν-; the other, which I address at once, concerns the precise force of the adjectival termination -τος.

Verbal adjectives ending in -τος are very common in Greek. They are generally held to be ambiguous: V-τος may carry the notion of possibility and have a 'modal' sense ('can be V-ed') and it may also have an ordinary non-modal sense ('is V-ed'). The ambiguity was familiar to the Greeks themselves. Thus Galen carefully explains that the adjective αἰσθητός, which derives from the verb αἰσθάνεσθαι ('to perceive'), sometimes means 'perceivable' and sometimes 'perceived' (*diff puls* VIII 710 K). Hence we might conclude that ἀνεπίκριτος may mean either 'undecidable' or 'undecided' – 'there is no decision' for a dispute either if the dispute cannot be decided or if it has not been decided.

Yet this conclusion is too swift, and it ignores a further subtlety. Suppose there is a jewel at the bottom of the sea: can it be perceived? In a sense, plainly not. But this is precisely Galen's example of something which is αἰσθητός in the sense of 'perceivable'. So the jewel is perceivable even though it cannot be perceived. It can (in one sense) be perceived; it cannot (in another sense) be perceived. It is the sort of thing which, given the right conditions, is perceived; but now, the conditions being wrong, it cannot be perceived. In short, we must distinguish between something's being in principle perceivable and something's being in the circumstances perceivable.

Aristotle, like Galen, was alive to the ambiguities of adjectives terminating in -τος. Thus he comments on the adjective ἄφθαρτος, which derives from the verb φθείρειν ('to destroy'):

> 'It is now ἄφθαρτος' is ambiguous: it means either that it has not now been destroyed, or that it cannot be destroyed now, or that it is now such as never to be destroyed.
>
> (*Top* 145b24–7)

Here Aristotle notes a third sense in addition to the two distinguished by Galen. For 'It is ἄφθαρτος' ('There is no destruction for it') may mean either (i) 'It has not been destroyed', or (ii) 'It cannot (in the circumstances) be destroyed', or (iii) 'It is not the sort of thing to admit destruction'.

Thus if we said of a problem that it was ἄλυτος ('There is no solution for it'), we might mean either (i) that it has not been solved, or (ii) that it cannot at the moment be solved, or (iii) that it is genuinely insoluble. And a διαφωνία may be ἀνεπίκριτος inasmuch as (i) it has not been decided, or (ii) it cannot at the moment be decided, or (iii) it is not in principle decidable.

Most Sextan scholars seem to take the word ἀνεπίκριτος in the strongest sense, sense (iii). Now there are passages in which Sextus explicitly says that a disagreement *cannot* be decided, or that it is not *possible* to decide a disagreement.[21] These passages could indeed be read in sense (iii). Moreover, any reader of Sextus is likely to derive the impression that, if the Pyrrhonists are right, disagreements are simply and in principle undecidable. But the impression may be misleading; and the texts, important though they are for determining the Pyrrhonian attitude to certain disagreements, do

21 See *PH* I 26, 29, 59, 178; II 85, 113, 116, 181; III 54.

not thereby determine the *sense* of the word ἀνεπίκριτος. For, evidently, one could hold that a disagreement was undecidable or not the sort of thing to be decided, and yet, in calling it ἀνεπίκριτος, mean only that it was undecided. Your attitude to διαφωνία does not in itself fix the sense you assign to the word ἀνεπίκριτος. And there is in fact some reason to suppose that in Sextus' writings the adjective ἀνεπίκριτος should not be interpreted in sense (iii).

For on more than one occasion Sextus says that a dispute is ἀνεπίκριτος *up to now*, or that it is *still* ἀνεπίκριτος, or that it *awaits* decision.[22] The implication is that, for all the sceptic knows, the disagreement *might*, in the future, be resolved. Now it would be at best mildly odd to say that a disagreement is 'still' or 'up to now' not the sort of thing that can be decided. If something is ever not the sort of thing to be decided, it is surely always not the sort of thing to be decided. Modal status of this sort does not change. (Similarly, it would be odd to say 'It is, up to now, impossible to be at the same time both taller and shorter than someone else'.) Hence in these passages we should be inclined to take ἀνεπίκριτος in sense (i) or sense (ii); an ἀνεπίκριτος διαφωνία is a disagreement which remains undecided or which no one has yet managed or been able to decide. And if in these passages, why not in all passages?

Sense (i) or sense (ii)? Some passages seem to me to favour (i) and others to favour (ii), and I cannot decide if it is right to fix upon one of these senses for all the occurrences of the word in Sextus. None the less, I have chosen to translate the adjective by 'undecided', as though it always bore sense (i). Even if this is mistaken, it is not an important mistake; for as a matter of fact the difference between (i) and (ii) does not affect any of the arguments in which the adjective crucially occurs. Thus if we think of an ἀνεπίκριτος διαφωνία as an undecided dispute, we shall avoid the serious error of imagining that such disagreements in principle cannot be resolved, and at the same time we shall not falsify the logic of any Sextan arguments.

---

22 For μέχρι (ἄχρι) νῦν (δεῦρο) see: *PH* III 70; *M* VIII 177, 257, 400, 427; XI 229; for ἔτι: *M* XI 230, 231; *M* I 28; II 95; for μένειν: *M* VIII 177, 187. Note also the phrases with ἐφ' ὅσον at *PH* III 3; *M* VII 380; VIII 118; and further the texts referred to in n.29 below. For what it is worth, I note that Caelius Aurelianus uses *iniudicatus* as (presumably) a translation of ἀνεπίκριτος: *morb acut* II 8.

Sextus does not always qualify the noun διαφωνία with the adjective ἀνεπίκριτος; but he does so very frequently,[23] and he also uses a number of other qualifying adjectives with the same general force.[24] It is plain, I think, that the mode from disagreement depends – in one of its forms, at least – on *undecided* disagreement. In other words, scepticism is supposed to follow not from the fact of disagreement as such but rather from the fact of undecided disagreement. Thus:

> The question proposed ... whatever it may be, is a subject of disagreement. Now will they say that the disagreement is decided or undecided? If undecided, we have it that we must suspend judgement. For it is not possible to make assertions about matters which are disagreed upon without decision (ἀνεπικρίτως). (*PH* I 170)

And so, explicitly, in some twenty-five further passages.[25] Thus 'as long as (ἐφ᾽ ὅσον) the dispute is undecided, we must remain in suspension of judgement' (*M* VIII 118).

Is this a good argument? It rests on the principle that, in Sextus' words, 'It is not possible to make assertions about matters upon which there is undecided disagreement'. But this principle cannot be literally true. For it is perfectly possible to make assertions on such matters. People *do* make positive assertions in the face of undecided disagreements (indeed the parties to the disagreements *must* do so); and if they do, they can. So we must modify Sextus'

---

23 See *PH* I 26, 59, 88, 98, 112, 114, 165, 170, 175, 178, 185; II 19, 29, 32, 33, 49, 57, 58, 59, 67, 85, 112, 113, 114, 116, 121, 145, 168, 181, 222, 259; III 3, 5, 6, 54, 56, 70, 108, 182, 254; *M* VII 341, 380; VIII 118, 177, 257, 265, 266, 288, 297; XI 230; *M* I 27; II 95, 102. (This list includes any use of ἀνεπίκριτος, adjectival or adverbial, in connexion with any word for disagreement.)

24 E.g. ἀνήνυτος (*PH* II 8, 31, 212; III 56; *M* VIII 262; *M* I 91, 156); ἄπειρος (*PH* II 48, cf. δι᾽ αἰῶνος: *M* VIII 186; *M* I 170); ἄσπειστος (*PH* III 175; *M* XI 36, see above, n.17); ἀδιάκριτος (*M* VIII 214); note also ἀμύθητος (*PH* II 21), ποίκιλος (*M* XI 217; *M* I 9), ἰσοσθενής (*PH* I 26; III 65, 139; *M* I 6), οὐχ ἡ τυχοῦσα (*M* V 37), μετέωρος (*M* I 28).

25 See *PH* I 26, 29, 59, 88, 112; II 19, 32, 57, 145, 259; III 5, 56, 108, 186, 254; *M* VII 380; VIII 177, 257, 265, 427/8; *M* I 170/1, 320; II 102; and cf. *PH* III 65, 139; *M* I 6 (διαφωνία ἰσοσθενής leads to ἐποχή). There is a twist to the story: often Sextus says that an undecided disagreement induces suspension of judgement; but sometimes he says that it leads to unknowability, ἀκαταληψία. On this, see above, pp.9–10.

principle. And clearly – or so we might suppose – the appropriate modification will refer not to possibility but to rationality, not to what we can or cannot say but to what we should or should not say. Then let us replace 'It is not possible' by 'One should not' (where the 'should' bears not a moral but an epistemological sense: 'It is not rational, or warranted, or justifiable . . .').

Sextus himself might not have been happy with this modification; for in general he prefers – and has reason to prefer – 'can' and 'cannot' to 'should' and 'should not'. (He will rather say that διαφωνία *causes* the πάθος of ἐποχή than that διαφωνία makes it *rational* for us to suspend judgement.) This preference raises difficult questions, both exegetical and philosophical. I ignore them here; for it is plain that, whatever Sextus might have said, we ourselves shall get no further with the principle enunciated at *PH* I 170 unless we reformulate it in terms of a rational 'should not'.

Even so, the reformulation is not enough to save the principle. For it seems clear that I may sometimes rationally make assertions where there is an undecided dispute. A student of ancient philosophy might rationally assert that the *Magna Moralia* was not written by Aristotle, even though there is (let us allow) an undecided disagreement about the matter. For, first, the student might be perfectly unaware of the disagreement and have no reason at all to suspect its existence. (He might possess good evidence for inauthenticity and no indication that the matter was controversial.) Or again, he might be aware of the disagreement and yet suppose – falsely, but for good reasons – that it had been decided. (He might, for example, have been falsely assured by a reputable scholar that the old διαφωνία had at last been settled.)

Thus we need a second modification to Sextus' principle: the principle should not connect suspension of judgement with διαφωνία *tout court* – it should connect suspension with *known* διαφωνία. Thus:

> If someone is aware that there is an undecided dispute about ?Q, then he ought not to accept or reject any proposed answer to ?Q.

I suppose that this thesis represents what the Pyrrhonists *ought* to say, even if they do not actually express themselves in this way. I shall refer to it as the Principle of Disagreement.

Disagreement

Now the question raised by the mode of disagreement is this: Is the Principle of Disagreement true? And the answer is surely: Yes, the Principle *is* true. For suppose that it were not true. Then the following could be the case. I recognize that there is a dispute about the authenticity of the *Magna Moralia*, some holding that the work was written by Aristotle himself and others holding that it is a later counterfeit. I believe, further, that the dispute is still undecided: the parties have not come to any agreement, and no decisive argument or consideration for or against authenticity has yet been advanced. Nevertheless (if the Principle is false) it is rational for me to hold that the work is not authentic. Now it seems clear to me that this is incoherent; for how could it possibly be rational for me to plump for authenticity, thus opting for one side to the dispute, and yet still to maintain that the dispute is undecided? If it is rational or warranted for me to decide against authenticity, then I must suppose that whatever warrants my decision also and thereby decides the dispute, which I can therefore no longer hold to be undecided. If, on the contrary, I insist that the disagreement remains undecided, then I cannot consistently suppose that my inclination to reject authenticity, whatever it may be founded upon, has any satisfactory justification; and hence it is not rational for me to reject authenticity.

Of course, I may adopt it as a 'working hypothesis' that the *Magna Moralia* is a counterfeit. I may act as if the work is spurious – say, by excluding it from my translation of the collected works of Aristotle. But in so acting I am not manifesting any *belief* that the work is spurious. I am not putting money on the horse. (Moreover, I may perhaps also hold that it is likely or probable that the work will turn out to be spurious. Then I shall indeed hold a belief on the matter – but not a belief which is, in any straightforward way, a party to the disagreement. For the disagreement is not over probabilities but over authenticity.) Thus while recognizing the existence of an unresolved dispute over authenticity, I may yet act as if the work is spurious (and perhaps even take it to be probably spurious); but I cannot rationally believe that it is spurious.

If this putative counter-example to the Principle of Disagreement is incoherent, then any putative counter-example is incoherent. And thus the Principle is true. Then since the Principle on which the mode of disagreement rests is true, the mode does indeed induce suspension of judgement. If I recognize undecided dispute over ?Q, then I must – I rationally must – suspend judgement over the matter.

Thus Agrippa's mode ἀπὸ διαφωνίας embodies a sound principle. Agrippa, here at least, is right. Now while conceding victory to Agrippa, we might at the same time wonder how significant his victory really is – but before I air that notion, let me, by way of a diversion, mention two corollaries of the Principle of Disagreement. First, recall the distinction between (D1) and (D2), between disagreement in opinion and disagreement in attitude. The Principle of Disagreement allows us to prove a curious thesis about disagreement in attitude: any διαφωνία in attitude to which a sceptic is a party is always decided. For suppose that there is an undecided disagreement over ?Q, and that Sextus himself is a party to it. (In answer to the question ?Q, some say P and Sextus, of course, suspends judgement.) Since the διαφωνία is undecided, it follows by the Principle that we should suspend judgement over ?Q. Yet if we suspend judgement over ?Q, we are siding with one of the parties to the διαφωνία and therefore deciding it. In other words, the Principle requires us to resolve the dispute in Sextus' favour. And so, in this particular sort of case, the Principle leads to a decision.

Sextus sometimes speaks as if *all* διαφωνίαι are undecided – indeed, as I have said, he is often taken to suppose that all διαφωνίαι are in principle undecidable. But this cannot be right. Some disagreements of attitude are decidable, and are implicitly recognized as decidable – indeed, as decided – by Sextus himself. The thesis we may find in Sextus (if we may properly speak of 'theses' in connexion with a Pyrrhonist) is not the thesis that all disagreements are undecided but rather, and at best, the thesis that all disagreements *of opinion* are undecided.

The second diversionary point is this. The mode ἀπὸ διαφωνίας does not really depend on διαφωνία, and the Principle of Disagreement is not really a principle of disagreement. The Principle states that I must suspend judgement over ?Q if I am aware of an undecided dispute over ?Q, that is to say, if I am aware (i) that different people have taken different attitudes to ?Q, and (ii) that no decisive reasons have yet been adduced in favour of any answer to ?Q. Now it is plain, I think, that the Principle would remain true even if clause (i) were omitted; for what grounds and warrants the Principle is the connexion between suspension of judgement and the lack of decisive reasons – and it is clause (ii) which makes this connexion. Yet clause (ii) does not invoke the notion of dispute. Dispute is invoked only in clause (i), which is otiose.

Thus the mode from disagreement depends on the Principle of Disagreement. The Principle of Disagreement makes reference to διαφωνία, but it does so, as it were, accidentally. Hence it is only a superficial feature of Agrippa's first mode that it deals with disagreement. Essentially, the mode has nothing to do with διαφωνία. (But I shall, on good conservative principles, continue to talk of the mode of dispute or disagreement.)

Let me return to the earlier question. Agrippa, I said, wins a victory – but how much territory does he actually gain? There is a difficulty with the argument which I based on the Principle of Disagreement. The difficulty is not that the conclusion of the argument is false. Rather, it is that the conclusion is too obvious and commonsensical a truth. The Pyrrhonists advanced the mode from dispute as a way of inducing a radical scepticism; for it supposedly applies to 'any matter proposed' (*PH* I 165). But the mode, as we have thus far understood it, seems to offer a sober and cool-headed account of rational assent, and to be far removed from any extreme form of Pyrrhonism. Why, in that case, did the Pyrrhonists make such a fuss over the διαφωνία mode? The answer lies in their thought that there is 'undecided faction' on absolutely every topic (*PH* I 165), or, as Sextus puts it a little later, that 'things plain and things unclear are all of them disputed' (*PH* I 185), which is to say that *everything* is disputed. If there is undecided dispute about ?Q, I shall suspend judgement over ?Q. If there is undecided dispute over every topic, I shall suspend judgement over everything. Thus the Principle of Disagreement generates universal scepticism – provided that there is undecided disagreement everywhere.

But whyever concede that undecided dispute is ubiquitous? Why concede even that there has been dispute of any sort on literally *every* topic? After all, Sextus himself appears to allow that, in some cases at least, there may not, so far as we yet know, be any διαφωνία at all. Yet he is undisturbed by this seemingly damaging admission; for in such cases, he explains, we should reflect that there *might* be disagreement.

> If on some issues we cannot immediately produce an anomaly, then we should say that in some countries unknown to us it is possible that there is a disagreement even on these matters. (*PH* III 233)

And we might, I suppose, be prepared to grant that on any issue whatever, there may, for all we know, be a disagreement. For even if everyone I have ever come across takes a uniform attitude to some question or other, nevertheless other people in other places may just possibly, for all I know, take a different line.

Let us allow to Sextus, then, that on every issue there is, for all we know, a διαφωνία. Yet this concession is of no value to the Pyrrhonists. In granting it, we are only granting that there *may be* disagreement over every issue, that there is, if you like, *potential* disagreement over every issue. We are not granting that there is *actual* disagreement over every issue. Still less, of course, are we granting that there is *undecided* disagreement over every issue. But the Principle of Disagreement involves undecided dispute. Hence we shall not and should not allow that, by way of the Principle, the mode of διαφωνία yields universal scepticism. There are (we may still maintain) topics on which no dispute actually arises, and there are also topics on which any dispute that has arisen has already been decided. On these topics at least, so far as the mode of διαφωνία is concerned, we are at liberty to make non-sceptical assertions. The mode of disagreement may indeed, as we have seen, lead to local scepticisms. But it seems that it will at best produce a modest, urbane, bourgeois little scepticism. It will not yield the red radicalism of the Pyrrhonists.

If Sextus is to reach a red radicalism, he must somehow start from the assumption of disagreement *simpliciter* (or even of *potential* disagreement) and not from the assumption – implausble if extended to 'any matter proposed' – of undecided disagreement. And yet he must somehow also manage to make use of the Principle of Disagreement, which refers only to *undecided* disagreement. He must contrive to have it both ways. Now there are in fact several arguments in which Sextus contrives, or purports to contrive, to have it both ways. Some of these arguments involve other Agrippan modes, and in the last chapter of the book I shall consider, generally, the ways in which the Agrippan modes may work in collaboration to a sceptical end. But even if these arguments are successful, they will not show that the mode of disagreement by itself can induce radical scepticism. So for the present, let us restrict our attention to the mode of disagreement, and ask whether this mode, by itself, can possibly produce large-scale suspension of judgement. I shall look at one particular argument which purports to have just this outcome.

Fairly often, the Pyrrhonists do seem to think that they can argue from mere disagreement (rather than from undecided disagreement) to suspension of judgement, and that they can do this without invoking any other sceptical argument-forms.[26] The texts are not exactly probative – sometimes it may seem reasonable to 'understand' a qualifying ἀνεπίκριτος with the word διαφωνία, sometimes it may seem reasonable to think that Sextus is tacitly alluding to the adjunction of further argument-forms. But I think that in many of these texts it is most plausible to suppose that Sextus does wish to move from disagreement to suspension of judgement without qualification or ado. And Galen, in the passage from *Against Julianus* I cited earlier, implies that it is characteristic of the ἀπορητικός to take exactly this leap.

Can we explain, or even justify, the leap? Sextus frequently reminds us that if an issue is under dispute, then it is unclear or ἄδηλον,[27] and that we therefore need some criterion or sign or proof if we are to decide it.[28] It is puzzling that Sextus should profess that all matters subject to dispute are thereby 'unclear' or ἄδηλα; for he also expressly says, at *PH* I 185, that φαινόμενα, i.e. things which are *clear*, are subject to dispute. But Sextus' use of the term ἄδηλον is notoriously perplexing – and fortunately the point does not matter greatly here. For here the crucial claim is that where there is disagreement, there we require some criterion or sign

---

26 See *PH* I 163, 177; II 153; III 13, 197, 235, 238; *M* VIII 2, 353, 356; IX 191.

27 See e.g. *PH* II 116, 168, 182; *M* VIII 328, 334, 335; *M* II 108.

28 See e.g. *PH* II 172, 182; *M* VII 341, 346; VIII 178/82, 317, 341, 346, 351, 365, 430; XI 177. Also *PH* III 6, where an *undecided* disagreement is said to lead to ἀδηλότης and to require proof.

or proof; we require a mode or means of deciding the issue: we require, as I shall put it, a yardstick. And this claim must seem highly plausible. For what is the alternative? Only, it seems, an arbitrary decision to opt for one side of the dispute or another – and that can hardly count as a resolution of the dispute. There is disagreement over ?Q. Some hold that P_1, some that P_2. We wish to determine who, if anyone, is in the right; we want to decide which answer, if either, is true. And for that we need more than an arbitrary and capricious act of plumping. We require to master some means of deciding the issue. In Sextan terms, we need a criterion or a sign or a proof. We need a yardstick.

But, as Sextus himself insists at length in *PH* II and *M* VII–VIII, every attempt to produce a yardstick has been subject to deep disagreement. Our primary problem, ?Q, thus raises a secondary problem (or 'meta-problem'), viz.: How are we to decide ?Q itself? What is an appropriate yardstick in the case of ?Q? And this meta-problem is, according to Sextus, itself involved in undecided dispute. Thus every disagreement leads to a further disagreement, namely a disagreement over yardsticks, and this disagreement is itself undecided. But if the disagreement over yardsticks is undecided, then we surely cannot properly use a yardstick. Hence every dispute is undecided.

Sextus expresses the point like this: 'Surely the dispute among the philosophers over the highest things does away with knowledge of truth?' (*M* VII 369). The 'highest things' include, of course, criteria and signs and proofs. Sextus means that if you dispute over the procedures for judging disagreements, then everything else is indirectly involved in the dispute and hence a matter for suspension of judgement. The argument is given fairly explicitly in the following passage.

> There has been disagreement among the natural philosophers over all things, I suppose, whether objects of perception or objects of thought. And this disagreement is undecided, since we cannot use a criterion, whether an object of perception or an object of thought – for *everything*, whatever we take, is a matter of disagreement and hence lacks warranty. (*PH* I 178)

Note two things about this argument. First, it takes as its premiss a claim about the prevalence of disagreement, and not a claim about the prevalence of undecided disagreement. It supposes only that everything has been disputed – and perhaps the argument *need* only assume that everything is, for all we know, disputed. The argument starts not from undecided disagreement, but from ordinary disagreement – and perhaps it may start from potential disagreement. Secondly, the only sceptical mode which the argument requires is the mode from disagreement, a mode which, I have argued, relies, in one of its applications, on an indisputably sound Principle. Thus if the argument works, then it establishes a radical, general scepticism from disagreement alone, without invoking either undecided disagreement or any supplementary Agrippan modes.

Sextus' argument at *PH* I 178 is, I think, interesting and important. I want to set it out as formally and as rigorously as I can. In doing so, I shall tacitly modify or emend Sextus' statements at a few points; but I think the version I offer can decently be called an interpretation of Sextus' words. Here, then, is the Sextan argument in white tie and tails.

(1) On every issue ?Q there has been (or might be) disagreement
(2) If a disagreement is to be decided, then we need a yardstick to decide it
(3) If we are to use yardstick Y for issue ?Q, we must be justified in holding that Y is appropriate for ?Q
(4) On any question of the form 'Is Y appropriate for ?Q?' there is undecided disagreement

Hence, from (4) by the Principle of Disagreement:

(5) For no Y and no ?Q are we justified in holding that Y is appropriate to ?Q

Hence, by (3) and (5):

(6) For no Y and no ?Q may we use Y for ?Q

Hence, by (1) and (2) and (6):

(7) No issue is decided

Hence, by the Principle of Disagreement again:

(8) On every issue ?Q, we should suspend judgement.

When an argument is set out as fussily as this, it should be easy enough to see where its faults are – if it has any faults.

We could always reject premiss (1), but this would be a tedious option. For we shall surely grant, as a plain empirical truth, that almost all important issues, as well as most minor issues, have in fact been subject to disagreement. Thus even if we rejected (1), we should still, as far as the rest of the argument goes, find ourselves reaching a disquietingly Pyrrhonian conclusion. For we should have to replace (1) by a modification which would be strong enough to induce scepticism over almost all major and most minor issues. We should not end up as radical sceptics, but we should be left believing nothing of interest or importance.

As for premiss (2), I have already argued for it; and I think we should accept it as a truth about rationality.

Again, the logic of the argument seems impeccable. From step (4) onwards there is nothing to question.

Hence in order to avoid something close to radical Pyrrhonism we must reject premiss (3) or premiss (4) or both. And indeed both these premisses are questionable. I shall end this chapter with some inconclusive reflections upon them.

First, what of premiss (4)? Are there really undecided disagreements about every yardstick? Sextus himself argues at considerable length to the effect that there are undecided disputes about the criterion of truth and about signs and proofs; but these arguments I shall ignore here, for they adduce other sceptical argument-forms, and the interest of the present argument lies precisely in the fact that it appears to argue from disagreement to scepticism without adducing any other forms of sceptical argumentation. Of course, Sextus' other arguments may be sound; and then he will be able to defend (4). But that is not my present concern.

In any case, (4) looks as though it is meant to be construed as an empirical premiss. The people who have thought about yardsticks are – or, in Sextus' time, were – philosophers; and they habitually disagree among themselves, never more so than over the criterion of truth and the theory of signs and proofs. So I think we may allow it to be true that on every question of the form 'Is Y appropriate to ?Q?' – on every question of this form which had been raised – there had been philosophical disagreement.

But was the disagreement undecided? (For premiss (4) essentially demands that the disputes over yardsticks be undecided.) Here we need to attend more closely to the notion of decision, which I have so far used without any particular explanation. We need to answer the question which I earlier postponed: What is the force of the verbal root ἐπικριν- in the adjective ἀνεπίκριτος?

In supporting premiss (4), Sextus might think to offer us the following simple reflection: Epicureans and Stoics have been in dispute for years over the criterion of truth, the Epicureans advancing and the Stoics rejecting the sovereign claims of sense-perception. The dispute still rages, neither party being prepared to concede an inch to the other. Thus plainly the disagreement is undecided – were it decided (say, in the Stoics' favour), then one party (here the Epicureans) would have thrown in the sponge.

The notion of decision involved in this little argument is closely connected with the notion of persuasion. In this sense of 'decide', a dispute is decided when and only when the parties to it come to an agreement or form a consensus – when, instead of a 'truceless war', there is a peace treaty signed and ratified by all the belligerents. There is, I think, little doubt that Sextus sometimes has this notion of decision in mind. For example (the context is irrelevant):

> If this is to be agreed upon, there must first be a consensus and an agreement among all the natural philosophers about the existence of perceptible objects . . . But there has been no consensus. Rather,
>   as long as water flows and tall trees flourish[29]
> the natural philosophers will never cease from warring with one another on the matter.   (*M* VIII 183–4)

Here the disagreement is plainly construed as an actual, historical dispute among the philosophers; and agreement or decision – the settlement of the disagreement – is construed as a sort of peace treaty to which each warring party is a signatory and by which each party binds itself to a common view. Let us call this sort of decision – for want of a better phrase – *historical* decision.

Now if we think of decisions in this way, it seems clear that there *is* undecided dispute over pretty well every issue about yardsticks. Perhaps *some* disputes have been, in this sense, settled – this is an historical question to which I do not know the answer. But it is plain that all the chief problems – I mean, all the chief philosophical problems – remain historically unresolved, in the sense that no

---

29 The line, from an anonymous epigram on Midas (see Plato, *Phaedrus* 264D), is quoted again by Sextus, in similar contexts, at *PH* II 37 and *M* I 28.

school has ever persuaded all the members of every rival school to accept its views. (And in Sextus' time, as I indicated at the beginning of this chapter, it was a famous fact that philosophers never came to any agreements with one another.)

But it is also clear that historical decisions are not the sort of decision which bears upon the mode of disagreement and its sceptical claims – they are not the sort of decision which the Principle of Disagreement invokes. Suppose I am interested – again – in the problems of the *Magna Moralia*. I know that there has been a serious disagreement over the matter, and I know that the partisans of authenticity still write articles against the partisans of spuriousness, and *vice versa*. The disagreement has received no historical decision. No peace treaty has been signed. Recognizing this fact, am I rationally obliged to suspend judgement on the question? Evidently not. For I may well say something like this: 'The two sides are still quarrelling. But the issue has been decided – for someone has in fact produced decisive arguments in favour of spuriousness, whether or not the partisans of authenticity are ready to recognize it.'

In thinking in this way I employ a different notion of decision from the one I sketched before. A disagreement can be decided, in this second sense, even if all parties to it continue the fight. (And conversely, a disagreement may remain undecided in this sense even if the parties to it have all signed a binding treaty of agreement.) For the διαφωνία is decided (in this sense) just in case sufficient reason has been produced to determine that P_1 (say) is the correct answer to ?Q. In considering whether a dispute is, in this sense, decided, I shall not be particularly interested in the *attitudes* of the parties (except insofar as these attitudes may be evidence for the existence of plausible arguments on each of the conflicting sides); rather, I shall be concerned with the *arguments* for and against rival answers to ?Q. And I shall regard the dispute over ?Q as decided – whatever the parties to it may think – just in case among these arguments I find one which determines the issue in one direction or another. Call such decisions *rational* decisions.

It is evidently rational decision which is relevant to scepticism (and which I implicitly used in stating and arguing for the Principle of Disagreement). And it is clear, too, that it is rational decision which Sextus often intends when he uses the verb ἐπικρίνειν and its cognates. Should we then say that ἐπικρίνειν is ambiguous, sometimes meaning historical decision and sometimes rational? I am unsure; but I incline to think that ἐπικρίνειν always *means* 'decide' in the rational sense, but that Sextus sometimes – and misleadingly – pictures or dramatizes a rational decision as an historical decision.

However that may be, it is very far from plain that, in *this* sense of 'decide', premiss (4) of our Sextan argument is true. Have no disagreements about yardsticks been rationally decided? Has no determining reason ever been produced for any dispute over yardsticks? At the very least, we shall need some good reason to affirm premiss (4) – it cannot simply be accepted as a highly plausible empirical conjecture. Now Sextus does, as I have said, argue for (4); but his arguments appeal to other sceptical modes, and to the extent that they are needed to support (4), to that extent the argument before us does not show that διαφωνία by itself can induce scepticism.

I shall not positively assert that premiss (4) is false. But I do say that it demands special support from other Pyrrhonian arguments if it is to be made at all plausible. And in that case, as I have said, the argument loses its *special* appeal.

Finally, what of premiss (3)? This is, I think, the most interesting part of the argument. Let me repeat the proposition:

(3) If we are to use yardstick Y for issue ?Q, we must be justified in holding that Y is appropriate to ?Q

We can usefully distinguish two 'parts' to this premiss, thus:

(3*) If I am to use Y for ?Q, then
    (a) I must believe that Y is appropriate to ?Q, and
    (b) that belief must be justified

Now we shall surely agree that if part (a) of (3*) is required, then part (b) must be required too. Otherwise we should be maintaining that, if we are to use Y, then (a) we absolutely must *believe* that Y is appropriate and yet (b*) we need not be *justified* in that belief. That seems absurd. How could my using Y depend essentially on a belief about Y but yet be indifferent to the justifiability of the belief? Suppose I do believe that Y is appropriate to ?Q, but hold this belief because I read it in the tea-leaves, or because I fallaciously inferred it from a set of false premisses, or because it was suggested to me under hypnosis by a malignant hypnotist or . . . None of this need matter a hang (we are supposing) so long as I *have* the belief. But plainly it does matter a hang. Well, that is rhetoric, not argument; but I find it persuasive rhetoric, and I do suppose that to maintain (3*a) and deny (3*b) would be paradoxical.

But what of (3*a)? Should we accept this part of (3) as a truth? Plainly, someone might *in fact* use Y for ?Q without holding that Y is appropriate for ?Q. He might use Y without realizing that he is using Y, and *a fortiori* without having any opinions about its appropriateness for ?Q. Or he might be aware that he is using Y and yet never have considered the question of whether Y is appropriate to ?Q. A commonplace example of the first kind of case: we all use certain basic logical schemata in testing ordinary arguments; but few of us are aware that we are using these procedures; few of us use them selfconsciously. (As John Locke said, God did not make men bare two-legged creatures and leave it to Aristotle to make them rational. Aristotle codified, for the first time, certain logical procedures; yet men had been using such procedures, correctly but unconsciously, for centuries.) An example of the second kind: when I wanted to get an outside line on my old college telephone, I used regularly to depress a button marked 'Recall' before dialling the number. I do not know why I followed this procedure, but I followed it consciously. A colleague once saw me phoning and asked me why I was depressing the button. I realized that I had never really thought of the matter – I certainly did not actually believe that depressing the button was an appropriate (part of) the procedure for getting an outside line. (And in fact it was not.)

Thus it seems clear that believing Y to be appropriate for ?Q is not a necessary condition for using Y for ?Q. Is it a necessary condition for *justifiably* using Y for ?Q? It is not clear that it is. For suppose that Y is in fact the appropriate procedure for ?Q, then – even if I have no beliefs about Y at all – may I not be justified in using Y for ?Q, and justified precisely because Y *is* appropriate? Let me try to make the point absolutely plain. Sextus supposes, in his premiss (3), that

> If you are to use Y for ?Q, you must have reason to believe that
> Y is appropriate to ?Q

The counter-suggestion, which we may imagine being advanced by a Dogmatist, is this:

> You may be justified in using Y for ?Q provided that Y is in fact the correct means of deciding ?Q; you do not also need to *believe* that Y is appropriate to ?Q.

Is the counter-suggestion correct? If it is, then premiss (3) is false, and the Sextan argument from διαφωνία fails.

The Sextan supposition and the Dogmatic counter-suggestion together raise – or so I believe – a problem which lies at the heart of all epistemological reflection. I shall say no more about the problem here, but it will re-emerge at the end of the final chapter.

One further turn to the story. Suppose that – prompted by Sextus' argument – I *do* consider the question of the appropriateness of Y to ?Q. And suppose that either I decide that Y is not appropriate to ?Q or else I find myself in the sceptical position of not knowing whether Y is appropriate to ?Q. In *these* circumstances would I be justified in using Y for ?Q? Surely not. Or rather, surely I myself would not feel justified in using Y. Even if the Dogmatic counter-suggestion is correct, so that we may justifiably use Y without having reflected upon it, none the less once we *have* reflected on Y and found its credentials dubious, we shall surely not feel ourselves entitled to rely upon it.

Return, once more, to the *Magna Moralia*. This time suppose that I engage in stylometrical studies to determine the question of authenticity. Stylometry, I tacitly imagine, supplies a suitable yardstick for such questions of authenticity. But suppose next (what is, of course, highly likely) that someone raises the question of the appropriateness of current stylometrical methods to problems of authenticity. Suppose further (what is not implausible) that I decide that stylometrical methods are inappropriate to the problem, or else (more modestly) that I find it simply unclear whether or not stylometrical methods are appropriate. In these cases it seems plain that I shall not, and rationally cannot, continue to attack the problem of authenticity with stylometrical strategies. No doubt I may go on making stylometric tests – for fun, perhaps, or because I can think of nothing else to do, or in the hope that they may eventually turn out to be appropriate after all. But I can hardly suppose that I am *justified* in using stylometrical methods to determine the authenticity of the *Magna Moralia*.

If this last thought is right, then even if premiss (3) of the Sextan argument is false, we can readily find a suffect which is true, namely:

(3 +) If we are to use Y for ?Q, then it must *not* be the case that, having considered the question 'Is Y appropriate to ?Q?', we return a negative or a sceptical answer to it

Now proposition (3 +) is weaker than (3). It is not strong enough to sustain the Sextan argument from disagreement as it stands – I mean, it cannot replace (3) in the argument and provide the same logical power as (3) provided. So I do not offer it to the Pyrrhonist as a simple way of repairing the argument from disagreement. But (3 +) has an interest of its own. And it lies here as a warning to the Dogmatist; for it exemplifies a form of reflection which will turn out to be the final cunning thought in the Pyrrhonian philosophy.

Infinite regression

Zeno of Elea was the first philosopher to spin puzzles from the notion of infinity. Thereafter, thinkers of every persuasion were obliged to perpend the paradoxes of the infinite. They were also ready to use the concept of infinity in destructive arguments. And they were particularly fond of threatening any view opposed to their own with an infinite regression. Here are two characteristic examples.

Nemesius ascribes the following argument to the Platonist philosopher, Ammonius Saccas. Ammonius has argued that all bodies, being essentially divisible, require something to conserve them or hold them together, and that this conserving or containing force is properly called 'soul'. Well then, Ammonius asks, can souls themselves be corporeal?

> If the soul is a body of any sort, however rarefied, there will again be something to hold *it* together (for it was proved that every body requires something to hold it together). And so *ad infinitum* until we come to something incorporeal.
>
> (*nat hom* 70 M)

If the soul is a body, it must itself be conserved by another soul. This second soul, being *ex hypothesi* corporeal, will again be conserved by yet a third corporeal soul. And so on. Thus we shall have an infinite sequence of corporeal containing souls. But that – or so Ammonius assumes – is absurd. Therefore the soul is incorporeal.

Again, in his *Elementary Theory* the astronomer Cleomedes argues that there is a vacuum or void outside the cosmos, and wants to prove that it is of infinite extension. One of his arguments runs as follows. Were the extracosmic void finite in extent, it would be bounded by something. Not by body, since by definition all body is included in the cosmos. Hence by something incorporeal; and the only possible candidate among incorporeal things is void.

> Thus there will have to be another void containing the extracosmic void. And this, not being infinite, will have to be contained by another; and that by another, *ad infinitum*. Thus if we are unwilling to allow that the void outside the cosmos is infinite, we shall be reduced to the necessity of supposing infinitely many different voids – and that is utterly absurd. Hence we must agree that the void outside the cosmos is infinite. *(disc cycl* I i 8)

The example is pretty; for Cleomedes adduces the absurdity of a regressive infinity to show the necessity of a non-regressive infinity – since there cannot be an infinite sequence of distinct vacuums, the one vacuum must be of infinite extent.

Destructive arguments from infinite regression work in the following way. (1) We hypothesize the claim which the argument is intended to destroy (the claim that souls are corporeal or that the extracosmic void is finite). (2) From this hypothesis we next generate, by some process of inference, an infinite sequence of objects (an infinite sequence of souls or of voids). (3) We deny the possibility of such a sequence. And hence (4) we reject the hyothesized claim.

Note that the sequence generated at stage (2) is literally infinite: it is not merely very long, nor merely unimaginably long – it is infinitely long. (It contains as many members as there are positive integers: its members may be paired one to one with the integers in the infinite sequence ⟨1, 2, 3, ...⟩.) Now it is not true – nor did any ancient philosopher suppose – that *any* infinite sequence will suffice to ground an argument from infinite regression; for there are infinite sequences against which no objection can be raised. (The sequence of positive integers is infinite. But not even Aristotle, the most notable ancient opponent of the infinite, thought that there was anything disreputable about this sequence.) Yet equally, not all infinite sequences are tolerable, and where a sequence is intolerable a *reductio ad infinitum* – I mean, an argument of the form I have just described – may prove a sound and powerful device.

In ancient texts, the claim which is to succumb to an infinite regression often has an epistemological content – it is a claim to the effect that a certain proposition or type of proposition can be established or proved or known in a certain way. Thus a later Ammonius employs an epistemological regression in arguing that 'hypothetical' syllogisms cannot by themselves suffice for the presentation of ἀποδείξεις or proofs. By a 'hypothetical' syllogism Ammonius here means an argument with two premisses, of which one is a compound proposition (a conditional or a disjunction) and the other (called the 'extra assumption') a simple proposition. Now

> hypothetical syllogisms assume without proof what is called their further or extra assumption (and sometimes too their conditional or disjunctive component needs argument). Thus they need premisses to warrant their original premisses. Now consider how to establish *these* premisses: if you use another hypothetical syllogism, then you will need another way to establish the warrantability of *its* premisses, and another for *that*, and so *ad infinitum*, if you want to corroborate premisses by way of premisses.
>
> (*in Int* 3.19–26; cf. [Ammonius], *in APr* 67.11–15)

The claim which Ammonius examines is the claim that hypothetical syllogistic alone suffices to prove certain sorts of proposition. This claim, Ammonius argues, generates an infinite sequence of syllogisms in any putative proof; for each syllogism in the proof will contain at least one premiss which requires further support – and hence a further hypothetical syllogism. But such infinite sequences of syllogisms are impossible. Hence hypothetical syllogistic alone is not enough and a different form of argument – a 'categorical' syllogism – must be introduced in order to complete the proof and to block the threatening regression.

Ammonius' argument is formally parallel to that of his earlier namesake. Just as an incorporeal soul is required if an intolerable infinity of bodies is to be avoided, so a non-hypothetical syllogism is required if an intolerable infinity of hypothetical syllogisms is to be avoided.

Neither of the Ammonian arguments should seem immediately convincing – each makes some pretty questionable assumptions. But here I am concerned not to assess the soundness but only to display the form of the reasoning used by the two Ammoniuses. For this form of reasoning was especially dear to the Pyrrhonians. Regression *ad infinitum*, ἡ εἰς ἄπειρον ἔκπτωσις, grounded the second of the Five Modes of Agrippa – the second of the set of five argument-forms by the application of which the Pyrrhonians claimed to introduce universal ἐποχή or scepticism (*PH* I 166). And Sextus appeals, time and again, to infinite regressions in his arguments against the Dogmatic philosophers. The Dogmatists themselves use regression for Dogmatic ends – to refute an hypothesis and thereby establish its contradictory. The Pyrrhonians, of course, have no such designs: their regressions serve a sceptical purpose and introduce only ἐποχή.

The regressions in Sextus are not all of them epistemological; and some of Sextus' comments on his non-epistemological examples may aid our understanding of the epistemological cases.[1] But epistemological examples are – unsurprisingly – by far the more frequent. Sextus turns eagerly to regressions of proofs and regressions of criteria. If a philosopher offers a proof, he will then be required to prove the premisses of his proof, and the premisses of *that* proof, and so *ad infinitum*; or else he must prove the soundness of his first proof, and then the soundness of *that* proof, and so *ad infinitum*.[2] If a philosopher suggests a criterion of truth, he must produce a second criterion by which to show that the first criterion is adequate, and a third for the second, and so *ad infinitum*.[3] In a similar way, Dogmatic philosophers are entangled in infinite sequences of signs or of explanations or of definitions.[4] Sometimes the Dogmatic philosopher or his philosophy 'falls into infinity (ἐκπίπτειν εἰς ἄπειρον)'; sometimes the Pyrrhonist 'tosses' him there (ἐκβάλλειν). The result is the same: the Dogmatist disappears and the sceptic triumphs.

1 For non-epistemological regressions see: *PH* II 40; III 44, 67, 68, 76, 162; *M* VII 312; IX 221, 261, 435; X 20, 76, 139, 256; *M* I 180, 242/3; III 81. As the references suggest, and as we should in any case have guessed, such regressions are most common in the Pyrrhonian attacks on aspects of φυσική.

2 Sequences of proofs: *PH* I 122; II 85, 182; III 8, 36, 53; *M* VII 339; VIII 16, 21, 347; *M* II 109, 112.

3 Sequences of criteria: *PH* II 20, 36, 78, 89, 90, 92/3; III 36, 241; *M* VII 340, 429, 441; VIII 19, 78; cf. *PH* I 171, 172, 176; *M* VIII 28.

4 Sequences of signs: *PH* II 124, 128; of explanations: *PH* I 186; III 24; of definitions: *PH* II 207. See also *PH* I 179; *M* VIII 49–50.

There is a pleasing parody of the Pyrrhonian use of regression in Lucian.

> Imagine that we find someone who claims to know a proof and to be able to teach it to someone else – I suppose we shan't believe him without ado but shall look for someone who can judge if our man is speaking the truth. And if we are lucky enough to find such a person, it will still be unclear to us whether this arbiter knows how to distinguish good judges from bad; and we shall, I suppose, need another arbiter for this arbiter – for how could *we* know how to pick out a man who is good at judging? Do you see where this is leading? It's getting infinite and can't ever come to a stop and be grasped.
>
> (*Hermotimus* 70)

You are puzzled whether the first argument in Euclid's *Elements* is a sound proof. You call in an expert to pronounce on the question. But is the expert competent? Well, you had better call in a second expert to assess the competence of the first. And a third for the second. And so *ad infinitum*. Since you cannot consult an infinite series of experts, you cannot determine whether or not Euclid's argument is sound. Hence ἐποχή.

In his account of the Five Modes Sextus gives a brief description of his epistemological use of infinite regressions:

> In the mode deriving from infinite regression, we say that what is brought forward as a warrant for the matter in question itself needs another warrant, which itself needs another, and so *ad infinitum*. Thus we have nowhere whence to begin to establish anything, and suspension of judgement follows.
>
> (*PH* I 166)

(The description in Diogenes Laertius' parallel account, at IX 88, is briefer, and it adds nothing to what we learn from Sextus.)

The first application in *Outlines of Pyrrhonism* of the mode of regression is actually made before the mode has been officially introduced. According to the fifth of the set of Ten Modes ascribed to Aenesidemus, we shall be led to scepticism once we reflect on the fact that objects look different when viewed from different distances or in different places or in different postures. For we are thus confronted by a number of mutually incompatible appearances, and – so Sextus maintains – we cannot *prefer* one of the variant appearances and hold that it represents the real nature of the object. Now suppose that someone contests this, alleging that he can *prove* one appearance to be preferable to the others. What will Sextus say in reply?

> If he wants to use a proof, . . . then if he says that the proof is true he will be asked for a *proof* that it is true, and for another proof for that proof (for it, too, must be true), and so *ad infinitum*. (*PH* I 122)

Thus the Dogmatist holds that P (say, that Mount Vesuvius actually has the shape it appears to have from the Palazzo Tarsia), and he offers some reason R_1 in proof of P (say, that our eyes function most accurately when they are at a certain distance from the objects of vision). His claim is that R_1 establishes P. But this claim – or so Sextus alleges – opens up an infinite regression. For the dogmatist must next offer some further reason, R_2, to prove that R_1 is a true proof of P (he must show that the claim about our eyes really does support the claim about Mount Vesuvius); and then he must find a further reason, R_3, for R_2 and so on. Thus he must offer a sequence of reasons, $\langle R_1, R_2, \ldots, R_n, \ldots \rangle$, where each R_i shows that its predecessor is a true proof. The sequence is infinitely long. But there cannot be such an infinite sequence. Therefore the Dogmatist cannot prove that P by adducing R_1.

I shall not comment on the soundness of Sextus' argument at *PH* I 122. I cite it to illustrate the regressive mode in action. It is, from a formal and stylistic point of view, a typical example; and there is no need to produce further illustrations. Rather, I shall concentrate in what follows on the two main philosophical questions which the mode of infinite regression raises. First, what exactly is *wrong* with infinite epistemological regressions? (Indeed, *is* there anything wrong with them as such?) Secondly, why should the discovery of such a regression lead us, as Sextus thinks it must, to a sceptical suspension of judgement? I take the questions in reverse order.

Let us grant, for the sake of the next stretch of argument, that infinite epistemological regresses are indeed unacceptable. Suppose that a philosopher makes some claim – say, that things really are the way they seem from nearby – and that he then supports this claim by a procedure which admittedly opens up an infinite regression. Should we therefore suspend judgement about his claim? Should we decline to believe that it is true and also decline to believe that it is false? Sextus does indeed sometimes appear to suggest that in such circumstances we should (or shall) end in scepticism. And that, after all, is surely what it means to say that the regressive mode is a mode of ἐποχή, a mode which induces suspension of judgement.

But it is evident that, in the supposed circumstances, we should not and would not automatically suspend judgement – and for a trivial enough reason. Although our philosopher may have failed to make out a case for his claim, there may yet *be* a case, and someone else may have argued for the claim in a way which avoids any regression. The fact that one man produces a bad argument for the claim that P is in itself no reason at all for suspending judgement about the claim. It is a reason for criticizing the claimant, but it is no reason for doubting his claim. (If Sextus' argument at *PH* I 122 is sound, then we shall infer that a Dogmatist cannot prove P by adducing R_1. Evidently, we cannot make the further inference that we must suspend judgement over P. For the fact that one Dogmatist has made a hash of his defence of P does not show that there is no reason to believe P. Equally, of course, it does not show that there is no reason to reject P and to believe not-P.)

Hence it would be absurd to think that the mode of regression in and by itself is sufficient to produce ἐποχή. I do not like to think that Sextus really entertained this absurd thought. Rather, we should make, and we should suppose that Sextus makes, a hypothetical or conditional claim for the sceptical powers of the regressive mode. What I mean is this. If the *only* consideration offered in support of a given claim leads to an unacceptable epistemological regression, then we must suspend judgement on the claim. The regression induces scepticism not absolutely but hypothetically; for it induces scepticism on the hypothesis that no other, nonregressive, mode of support is available.

There is another way of expressing more or less the same point. If our Dogmatic philosopher, maintaining that P, offers us an argument which opens up a regression, then *as far as that argument goes* we shall and should suspend judgement. This particular argument cannot move us from ἐποχή – as far as *it* is concerned, we must be sceptical.

The phrase I have just used, 'as far as this goes', is common in

Sextus' writings. The Greek for it is ὅσον ἐπὶ τούτῳ (ὅσον ἐπὶ τοῖς λεγομένοις, τῷ λόγῳ, etc.).[5] And I suppose that Sextus' general view about the regressive mode is this: if you are given a regressive argument for a claim, then ὅσον ἐπὶ τούτῳ you will suspend judgement about that claim. Admittedly, I can produce no text in which Sextus actually says this; but his normal sceptical procedure implicitly shows that it was in fact his view. For normally the regressive mode is used not alone but in concert with other argumentative strategies. Schematically: someone urges that P. Sextus replies: 'If your claim that P is warranted, then either X or Y or Z. But X leads to an infinite regression, and Y and Z are unacceptable for different reasons. Hence your claim is unwarranted, and we shall suspend judgement.' Plainly, within such a strategy, the mode of regression has hypothetical force: as far as *it* is concerned, suspension of judgement must follow; if nothing else is to hand, we must suspend judgement.

We can thus see – and it is worth insisting – that the mode of regression and the mode of disagreement relate to suspension of judgement in rather different ways. And on two counts. First, as I have just explained, the regressive mode will rarely, if ever, produce ἐποχή on its own; for we shall rarely, if ever, be confronted by a claim for which the *only* argument (or counterargument) is an infinite sequence of reasons. By contrast, the mode of disagreement, as I explained in the previous chapter, is supposed to be capable of inducing ἐποχή by itself. Διαφωνία is, both in principle and in practice, often an independent worker. Regression, in principle normally and in practice always, works as one of a gang.

Secondly, and more interestingly, the regressive mode collaborates to induce scepticism not in virtue of its peculiar regressive character but rather in virtue of the fact that infinitely regressive arguments are (we are supposing) *bad* arguments. For if I am right, the principle behind the regressive mode is in fact a wholly general principle. It is the principle that if the only arguments for or against P are bad arguments, then we must suspend judgement over P. And the mode of regression helps to induce suspension just insofar as regressive arguments are bad arguments. Contrast the mode of disagreement: here it is the fact that there is undecided

5 See Karel Janáček, *Sextus Empiricus' Sceptical Methods* (Prague, 1972), pp.13–20.

disagreement – and not some more general fact of which undecided disagreement is one particular example – which of itself leads to ἐποχή. In these two ways, the mode of disagreement and the mode of regression are not on a level with one another.

In the final chapter I will say something about the way in which the mode of regression may collaborate with other sceptical procedures. Here I content myself with a highly hypothetical statement about the relationship between regression and suspension of judgement: if (i) arguments which generate an epistemological regression are unacceptable arguments, and (ii) the only argument we have for a given claim is such a regressive argument, and (iii) the claim should not be accepted without argument, then we should suspend judgement and remain staunchly sceptical about the claim. I believe that this highly hypothetical statement represents what Sextus ought to say, and perhaps what he means to say, about the connexion between infinite regression and scepticism. I also believe that the highly hypothetical statement is true. (Indeed, I suppose that it is little more than a tautology.)

But what of the first of the two questions I posed a while ago? Are regressive arguments unacceptable? And if so, why are they unacceptable? In other words, is the first hypothesis – clause (i) – in my highly hypothetical statement a true hypothesis? And if so, why is it true?

When he employs the regressive mode and points to an infinite regression, Sextus usually leaves unspoken the thought that infinite regressions are Bad Things. Occasionally he will note explicitly that a regress is 'impossible' without explaining why (e.g. *PH* I 122; II 182). But one objection to epistemological regressions is in fact briefly stated in his description of the regressive mode itself:

> Thus we have nowhere whence to begin to establish anything
> (μὴ ἐχόντων ἡμῶν πόθεν ἀρξόμεθα τῆς κατασκευῆς), and
> suspension of judgement follows.   (*PH* I 166)

In an infinite sequence we have no starting-point, nowhere πόθεν ἀρξόμεθα; for such sequences, as he says elsewhere, have no ἀρχή or are ἄναρχοι.[6]

---

6 See *PH* III 68, 76; *M* VII 312; VIII 78; X 76, 139, 256; *M* I 180, 242/3.
The thought is not peculiar to Sextus: see e.g. Aristotle, *Phys* 256a16.

Sextus puts the point most clearly in connexion with a non-epistemological regression. In *PH* III he considers the suggestion that bodies move insofar as each of their parts moves in sequence. (When a train starts to move, first the locomotive moves and then each of the carriages moves in sequence.) Against this suggestion he says:

> If bodies, and the places and times in which bodies are said to move, are infinitely divisible, then there will be no movement; for in infinite sequences (ἐν ἀπείροις) it is impossible to find any first element, from which what is said to move will first move.[7]   (*PH* III 76)

In an infinite sequence there is no *first* element. But if a body moves by virtue of the sequential movement of its parts, then its *first* part must move first, and so it must have a first part. Similarly, we may suppose, if a Dogmatic philosopher is to establish a claim by virtue of producing a sequence of supporting claims, then he must first produce the *first* such claim – and hence there must *be* a first claim. But in an infinite sequence of claims there is no first claim. Thus, on these suppositions, bodies will not move and claims will not be established.

The objection to Sextus' argument is plain: it is simply false that an infinite sequence must lack a first member. The sequence of natural numbers, $\langle 1, 2, 3, \ldots \rangle$, is infinite; its first member is 1. A train of infinitely many carriages none the less has a first part, viz. the locomotive, and the locomotive will be the first part of it to move. And our philosopher's putative sequence of arguments will also have a first member, namely the argument which has as its conclusion his claim that P. Thus in the case imagined at *PH* I 122, the first element in the infinite sequence of reasons is R_1.

Sextus might reply that this is to invert the natural order of things: if I am to establish P by way of R_1, then I must settle R_1 *before* I assert that P; and similarly I must settle R_2 *before* I settle R_1, and so on. Hence the first shall be last: the ἀρχή of the sequence, the item I must start from, is the *last* element in the sequence – but the sequence has no last element.

Now it is indeed true that the sequence $\langle R_1, R_2, \ldots, R_n, \ldots \rangle$ has

---

7 I read ἀφ οὗ πρῶτον κινήσεται (the MSS have πρώτου, not πρῶτον).

no *last* member. But is it true that in order to establish P I must begin from a last member of the sequence? The question raises a number of tricky issues concerning the notion of establishing or justifying a claim, and also concerning the relation of priority which this notion seems somehow to involve. These issues will exercise me in my next chapter. But I think that the immediate question can be answered fairly easily, without entering into these deeper issues. Let us consider a normal argument, consisting of a finite sequence of considerations. Suppose we have a proof of one of Euclid's theorems (call it theorem T). The proof can be represented as a finite sequence of arguments

$$\langle A_1, A_2, \ldots, A_n \rangle$$

where A_1 yields T as its conclusion, A_2 yields the premisses of A_1, and so on. The premisses of A_n are axioms or first principles of Euclid's geometry. (In real proofs matters are neither so linear nor so neat; but the additional complexities of real proofs do not matter here.) It is plain, I think, that in offering you a proof of T I may go through the arguments in this sequence in any order I like (or in any order you may find perspicuous). In particular, I may reason as follows: 'T is true, as you can see from A_1; and A_1 I support by A_2, and that by A_3, ... and that by A_n, the premisses of which are axioms of Euclidean geometry.' As far as I can see, there is no reason to hold that in arguing for T I *must* start from A_n, the last item in the sequence. But if that is so with a finite sequence, why may it not also hold of the infinite sequence $\langle R_1, R_2, \ldots, R_n, \ldots \rangle$? Why may I not happily start the infinite sequence from R_1? Thus Sextus' objection to infinite epistemological sequences does not work: as far as this objection goes, ὅσον ἐπὶ τούτῳ, there is nothing wrong with epistemological regressions; for we can in fact always find a starting-point for the argument.

Consideration of the schematic Euclidean proof will quickly suggest a second and quite different objection to infinite epistemological regressions. In the Euclidean case I supposed, of course, that I went through *all* the items in the sequence, that I produced each A_i in the sequence $\langle A_1, A_2, \ldots, A_n \rangle$. And here our Dogmatic philosopher's infinite sequence does seem to pose a problem. For although we may, as I have argued, easily discover a starting-point for our infinite epistemological journey, we shall hardly find a finishing-point. For how can we possibly go through or survey *every* member of an infinite series?

This objection to infinite epistemological sequences is no new invention. It was known to Aristotle, and he held it to be conclusive. In a celebrated chapter of the *Posterior Analytics*, to which I shall return, Aristotle reports briefly an argument used – we do not know by whom – to a sceptical end.

> These people claim that we are led back *ad infinitum*, since we cannot know the posterior items by way of the prior items if there are no primitive items. And here they are right; for it is impossible to go through infinitely many items.
>
> (*APst* 72b8–11)

We cannot properly sustain the claim that P by an infinite sequence of reasons $\langle R_1, R_2, \ldots, R_n, \ldots \rangle$; for no one can 'go through' or survey or produce such a sequence.

The objection, in its most general form, is a commonplace in ancient (and modern) thought: ἀδύνατον τὰ ἄπειρα διελθεῖν, it is impossible to survey an infinite set. Sextus himself applies it in more contexts than one. Suppose, for example, that when faced with a διαφωνία, you suggest that we should accept the opinion of the majority of men.

> Now there is an infinite number of individual men, and we cannot survey (ἐπελθεῖν) the judgements of *all* of them, and so assert what it is that the majority of all men assert and what the minority. (*PH* II 45)[8]

The case is curious (does Sextus really suppose that men are *infinite* in number?); but the objection and the general principle are clear. If we are to ascertain which view is the majority view, we must survey the whole class of men and count the number of votes in favour of each view. But there is an infinitely large class to survey – and we cannot survey an infinitely large class.

Sextus does once apply this objection to the matter with which I am primarily concerned. In the course of his sceptical attack on the notion of truth, he brings up the mode of regression in the following way:

8 See also *PH* II 89; *M* I 66, 224.

47

> If ⟨you try to show that something is true⟩ by way of a proof,
> we shall enquire again how you know that *this* is true, and so
> *ad infinitum*. Now since, in order to learn that something is
> true, you must first grasp infinitely many things, and it is
> impossible for infinitely many things to be grasped, it turns
> out to be impossible to know firmly that anything is true.
>
> (M VIII 16)

The standard Sextan objection to infinite regression – that no
starting-point is available – is not entirely lost sight of here; for the
claim that 'you must *first* grasp (προληφθῆναι) infinitely many
things' at least hints at the alleged impossibility of securing a *first*
point or ἀρχή. But the main weight in this passage evidently falls
elsewhere. The thought is that you cannot survey an infinitude of
propositions.

Now it may seem disappointing, or even perplexing, that Sextus
produces this objection only once, in *M* VIII 16, whereas the other,
bad, objection is, so it appears, his standard or official objection to
infinite epistemological regressions. For the objection of *M* VIII 16
may actually seem to be a good objection, an objection which really
does show that such sequences are unacceptable.

But is it a good objection? We shall surely grant that no one
can survey or produce each member in an infinite sequence. If I pur-
port to rest my claim that P on the sequence of reasons ⟨R₁, R₂, . . .,
Rₙ, . . .⟩, then I surely cannot produce or state or formulate *every*
Rⱼ. But how exactly does this impossibility validate the mode of regression? The objection plainly supposes that I must be able to produce or state or formulate *every* reason or argument in a sequence if
I am to base my claim on the sequence. But why should this be so?
Perhaps it just seems *obvious* that an appeal to a sequence of
arguments can be nothing other than an appeal to each and every
member of the sequence? Yet it is not clear to me that it is obvious.
And in fact the objection, as we have it so far, glosses over an
important distinction. An analogy will help to show what I mean.

The sequence of positive integers ⟨1, 2, 3, . . .⟩ is an infinite
sequence. Each member of the sequence has a unique (immediate)
successor (2 succeeds 1, 3 succeeds 2, . . ., 737 succeeds 736, . . . – and
so on, for ever). Neither I nor anyone else can name the successor of
every number in the sequence; neither I nor anyone else can in this
way survey the sequence or produce all its members. But there is

something else which I can do and which anyone who can count can do: we can each of us name the successor of *any* number. Give me any number whatsoever in the sequence, however remote, and I can at once name its successor. In this sense I *can* master the infinite sequence – nor is my mastery in the least bit idiosyncratic or remarkable.

The point is worth stating rigorously. There is something which I cannot do, viz. name the successor of every number, and something which I can do, viz. name the successor of any number. Thus we must distinguish between

> (1) It is possible that for every number *n* I name the successor to *n*

and

> (2) for every number *n*, it is possible that I name the successor to *n*.

The crucial difference between (1) and (2) is made by the difference in the relative order and scope of the modal operator ('it is possible that . . .') and the quantifying phrase ('for every number *n*'). In the most general and abstract case, there is a difference between

> (α) It is possible that for every x, x is F

and

> (β) For every x, it is possible that x is F

These two formulae are evidently different in their syntactic structure. They are also different – and this is the important point – in what they say. For they are not equivalent to one another. In particular, although if a formula of the form (β) is false, the corresponding formula of the form (α) must also be false, the converse is not the case: a formula of the form (α) may be false when the corresponding formula of the form (β) is true. In other words, formulae of the form (α) entail corresponding formula of the form (β), but not *vice versa*. A simple example should make the point clear. In a fair lottery with only one winning number it is false that

> (1*) It is possible that every number wins

but true that

> (2*) For every number, it is possible that that number wins.

Now sentence (2*) is of the form (β), whereas sentence (1*) is of the form (α). And that is how (2*) may be true while (1*) is false. Similarly, sentence (2) is of the form (β), whereas sentence (1) is of the form (α), and so (2) may be true while (1) is false.

I have laboured this point because it is easily and often overlooked. Once it is stated clearly, its truth will hardly be disputed. But unless it is stated it is liable to be ignored.

How does the distinction between (1) and (2), or between (α) and (β), apply to infinite epistemological sequences? The objection we are considering rests on the thesis, which is surely true, that we cannot survey every member of the whole infinite sequence of reasons or arguments. That is to say, it rests on denying a proposition of the form (α), a proposition formally analogous to sentence (1), viz. the proposition:

> (1a) It is possible that, for every reason R_i, I produce the next
> reason in the sequence, R_{i+1}, in support of R_i.

Now there is also a corresponding proposition of the form (β), a proposition formally analogous to sentence (2), viz. the proposition:

> (2a) For every reason R_i, it is possible that I produce the next
> reason, R_{i+1}, in support of R_i.

Just as we may consistently reject proposition (1) while accepting proposition (2), so we may consistently reject (1a) while accepting (2a).

Then my suggestion is this: although (1a) is false, its falsity is not sufficient to show that infinite epistemological sequences are unacceptable. For the acceptability of such sequences may (for all that has been thus far said) depend only on the truth of (2a). In other words, it may be enough if I can produce *any* reason in the sequence, even though I cannot produce *every* reason in the sequence. And, for all that has thus far been said, proposition (2a) may well, in some cases at least, be true. In other words, it may, in some cases, be possible for me to produce *any* reason in the infinite sequence. The objection to infinite regression rests on the denial of (1a). But this foundation is insecure. For the objection to succeed, it must not only reject (1a) but also reject (2a). And we have as yet been given no reason to reject (2a) in all its generality.

I believe that the preceding considerations are sound, and that they demonstrate the insufficiency of the good-seeming objection to infinite epistemological regressions. But how much is the demonstration worth? To what extent are infinite regresses thereby seriously defended? *Can* there be epistemological sequences for which (2a) is in fact true?

Consider again proposition (2). How is it possible that I can name the successor to any one of an infinite list of numbers? The answer is plain: I know a general way of constructing the successor to any number; I have – as the logicians say – an algorithm by which I can construct the successor to any number. For in order to construct the successor to n, all I need is the concept of *adding one*; since I have an entirely general grasp of this concept – of the operation denoted by '$\xi + 1$' – I can thereby name the successor to any number. It seems evident that my mastery of the infinite sequence depends upon – or consists in – my grasp of this algorithm; and it seems evident that in the absence of any algorithm of this sort I could not (except by magic) come to master an infinite sequence in the fashion of (2).

Thus infinite sequences of reasons will satisfy (2a) only if they are associated with some algorithm. If I have no general method for constructing R_{i+1} from R_i (no algorithm however complex), then – magic apart – I cannot hope to produce an R_{i+1} for every R_i.

At this point one matter – and a not unimportant matter – becomes plain. For it is plain that epistemological regressions are not epistemologically *serious* things. As a matter of fact, no philosopher has ever produced such a sequence, and no epistemologist has ever attempted to ground knowledge on infinite regressions. When Sextus refers, as he frequently does, to the threat of an infinite regression, the regressions are never given a detailed description – rather, Sextus merely gestures, in abstract terms, at the possibility, the theoretical possibility, of such a regression. And it is clear why this is so: in most of the cases which Sextus has in mind, there is no readily imaginable way of actually constructing the regression, because no appropriate algorithm can be conjured up.

Thus even if the Dogmatist is correct, as I have thus far argued, in holding that proposition (2a) is sufficient to ground the possibility of infinite epistemological regressions, he has gained very little. For unless he can also construct or find some appropriate algorithm, he cannot actually produce any infinite sequence which will do him epistemological service. The theoretical possibility of an acceptable regression is just that – an empty theoretical possibility.

None the less, regressions can in fact be constructed (at the price of some artificiality); and even if they are unlikely to be of any serious epistemological importance, they may still be interesting as theoretical possibilities. I offer two such sequences – indefinitely many others can readily be constructed on their model.

The first example is this. A mathematician claims that the number two is even. He supports this by arguing as follows:

> Four is even; and if four is even, two is even: hence two is even.

He supports the first premiss of *this* argument thus:

> Six is even, and if six is even, four is even: hence four is even.

And so on. Evidently, an infinite sequence of arguments is thus generated. Evidently, proposition (2a) holds of the sequence. For there is a simple algorithm for constructing any argument from its predecessor. (Suppose that one of the arguments in the sequence is 'n is even; and if n is even, then $n-2$ is even; hence $n-2$ is even'. Then the next argument in the sequence will of course be: '$n+2$ is even; and if $n+2$ is even, then n is even; hence n is even'.) Thus for *any* argument R_i in the infinite sequence, we can produce the supporting argument R_{i+1}.

The second example is slightly different. It is an attempt to meet the challenge issued by Sextus at *PH* 1 122, where the mode of infinite regression is first thrown down. A philosopher claims that P_1 (the content of the claim is immaterial). He supports the claim by a *modus ponens* argument:

> (R_1) If P_2, then P_1; and P_2: hence P_1.

And the sceptic challenges him to show that this argument is trustworthy. He replies by producing the following more complex argument:

(R_2) (i) If it is true that if if P_2, then P_1, and P_2, then P_1, then the argument 'If P_2, then P_1; and P_2: hence P_1' is acceptable. (ii) But it is true that if if P_2, then P_1, and P_2, then P_1. Hence (iii) the argument 'If P_2, then P_1; and P_2: hence P_1' is acceptable.

Now if the sceptic asks his opponent to warrant *this* argument, it is evident that he can do so by reapplying the same procedure to produce a yet more complex argument, R_3. And it is equally evident that the procedure will generate a sequence of infinitely many arguments. Each argument will be more complex than its predecessor. The second argument in the sequence – the one I have formulated – is not altogether easy to comprehend; and it would in practice be difficult and tedious to formulate even the third argument in the sequence. But the matter is in principle perfectly easy, and we can readily 'see' how the sequence is constructed.[9]

In each of these cases we have an infinite sequence of reasons or arguments; and the sequences can, in the defined sense, be mastered. No doubt the particular sequences I have constructed would not in fact be offered as proofs; and no doubt there are few if any such sequences which ever would be offered as proofs. But nevertheless, given that such sequences *can*, sometimes, be constructed, may they not in principle be offered as proofs? Have we not secured the *possibility* of an infinite epistemological sequence against which no objection can be made?

9 Each argument is in *modus ponens* form. Suppose that argument R_i is:

If A, then B; and A: hence B.

Then argument R_{i+1} will be:

If if if A, then B, and A, then B, then R_i is acceptable; but if if A, then B, and A, then B: hence R_i is acceptable.

The sequences of *if*s make this hard to grasp. A semi-symbolized version may make it a little easier. (The arrow stands for 'if . . ., then . . .', and the inverted V for '. . . and . . .' Thus R_{i+1} will be:

$(((A{\rightarrow}B) \wedge A){\rightarrow}B){\rightarrow}(R_i$ is acceptable)
$(((A{\rightarrow}B) \wedge A){\rightarrow}B)$
Hence R_i is acceptable.

(The example is based on a similar infinite sequence generated by Lewis Carroll in his classic paper, 'What the Tortoise said to Achilles', *Mind* 4, 1895, 278–80.)

You do not need to be a Pyrrhonist to be sceptical of all this: you may well feel there is something very fishy about the claim I have made for these infinite sequences. Even if it is admitted that such sequences will not, in practice, make any serious contribution to epistemology, you may still wish to urge that there is something more to be said – that they cannot, in principle, make any contribution at all. Can we show that this is right? And if so, can we explain why? I end with some tentative thoughts on these questions.

Look again at the first infinite sequence, to the conclusion that the number two is even. Call this conclusion P. The first argument was:

If four is even, then P; and four is even: hence P.

Call this argument R_1. We know how to construct R_2 and R_3 and R_4 . . . Thus we can marshall the following infinite sequence of arguments in support of P:

$$\langle R_1, R_2, \ldots, R_n, \ldots \rangle$$

Now imagine, in Pyrrhonian vein, a rival mathematician, locked in διαφωνία with the first. The rival strenuously maintains that the number two is odd, not even. Call this claim P*. The rival's first argument for P* is, of course, this:

If four is odd, then P*; and four is odd: hence P*.

Call this argument R^*_1. Plainly, the rival will be able to produce R^*_2 and R^*_3 and R^*_4 . . . Thus he can generate an infinite sequence of arguments in support of P*, viz.:

$$\langle R^*_1, R^*_2, \ldots, R^*_n, \ldots \rangle$$

His sequence, the P*-sequence, has exactly the same formal properties as the P-sequence; and it is constructed and mastered in exactly the same way.

Since the two sequences are exactly analogous to one another, then by 'parity of reason' the one will be epistemologically acceptable if and only if the other is. But P and P* are incompatible with one another. Hence *both* sequences cannot be acceptable. Hence *neither* sequence is acceptable. Hence the P-sequence is not acceptable.

The example can be generalized. For any infinite sequence Σ which we can construct, we may generate a rival sequence Σ^* with the following two properties: first, Σ^* is precisely analogous in form and structure to Σ; secondly, the claim purportedly warranted by Σ^* is inconsistent with the claim purportedly warranted by Σ. By virtue of the first property, either Σ and Σ^* are both acceptable or they are both unacceptable. By virtue of the second property, they are not both acceptable. Hence neither is acceptable. Hence Σ is not acceptable.[10]

Does this show that *no* infinite regressions can have any epistemological power? It is tempting to think so. But the argument is certainly less than probative. I mention two difficulties. First, is it true that an appropriate Σ^* can be constructed for any offered Σ? I do not know: the claim seems fairly plausible (at least, it is hard to see how one could construct a Σ for which one could not find a Σ^*); but I cannot prove that it is true. It is at best a tempting conjecture.

Secondly, even if an appropriate Σ^* is found, is the formal similarity between Σ and Σ^* enough to warrant the epistemological conclusion? Granted that Σ and Σ^* do not differ formally, are we then justified in holding that the one is epistemologically acceptable if and only if the other is? Perhaps the champion of infinite regressions will insist that Σ and Σ^* will, or must, differ in some non-formal way, and that this difference warrants his accepting Σ and rejecting Σ^*. And of course there *are* non-formal differences between Σ and Σ^*. In the particular case we are examining, there is an obvious and obviously pertinent non-formal difference between the two sequences. The elements in the P-sequence are all *true*, and the elements in the P*-sequence are some of them false. It is true that if four is even, then two is even; and it is true that four is even. It is (let us grant) true that if four is odd, then two is odd; but it is not true that four is odd. Hence despite their formal symmetry, the P-sequence and the P*-sequence are not on an epistemological par with one another.

'Ah', the sceptic will quickly reply, 'but we are trying to *prove* the truth of the elements in Σ and Σ^*. You cannot prefer one sequence to the other on the grounds that its elements are all true –

---

10 The general idea behind this line of argument, which the ancients would have called an ἀντιπαραβολή, was given to me by Stephen Everson.

that is to beg the question.' This is a neat rejoinder. But it is not plain that it is a just rejoinder. For after all, the proponent of the P-sequence is right and the proponent of the P*-sequence is wrong. And even if that does not – and cannot – give the proponent of the P-sequence a *reason* to prefer his sequence, it surely shows that he is *right* to prefer his sequence.

It is worth seeing precisely what is at issue here. The sceptic in effect urges that

> You may properly claim to know P on the basis of an infinite sequence of arguments Σ only if you have good reason to prefer Σ to any rival Σ*

– and given the formal identity between Σ and Σ*, you can never have good reason for a preference. The Dogmatist suggests rather that

> You may properly claim to know P on the basis of an infinite sequence of arguments Σ provided that the arguments in Σ are in fact good arguments; you do not need in addition to *know* that they are good arguments or to *know* that Σ is superior to any rival Σ*

– and hence the formal identity between the two sequences does not matter. Who is right here, the sceptic or the Dogmatist? The question is perplexing. It is similar to a question which arose at the end of the previous chapter and which I there postponed. The present question I also postpone to the final chapter.

Some of you, I suspect, have been losing patience with the last part of my discussion. Surely, you may be thinking, it is utterly plain both that and why infinite sequences are epistemologically absurd – they are absurd because they do not link our beliefs to *reality*. They embark on an endless succession of claims or beliefs, each of which ties down an earlier claim or belief, and each of which is tied down by a later claim or belief. But in order to prove or justify or warrant a belief or claim, it is not enough to tie it to other beliefs or claims. You must anchor it to the world, to reality. Beliefs must be linked or nailed or glued to what is *in fact* the case. (And then one might wonder if this is not really the very point Sextus is trying to make when he objects that infinite sequences give you no ἀρχή or starting-point. There is no ἀρχή to the sequence inasmuch as no item in the sequence takes us out of the realm of belief and into the realm of fact.)

I have often heard thoughts of this sort expressed. Like others, I find in them a Siren seductiveness. I am prepared to countenance the possibility that they voice the song which Sextus himself was trying to sing. I am even inclined to believe that there may be a truth towards which they are enticing us. But they do not succeed in voicing that truth themselves. For it is in fact easy to see how a Dogmatic proponent of infinite regressions will reply. 'Links with the world?' he will say, 'Of course beliefs must be linked with the world: whoever could deny *that*? But why on earth do you think that my infinite sequences have no worldly ties? Nothing could be further from the truth: P is itself linked to the world, i.e. it is true. Moreover, its link to the world is revealed and ensured by R_1. As for R_1, that too is linked to the world – for its premisses are true. And its worldly links are revealed and ensured by R_2. And so on. My sequence has *no* links with reality, do you say? Nonsense, it has infinitely many worldly links.'

The reply is just. To be 'linked to the world' is simply to be true of the world, i.e. to be true. Being linked to the world is not an *alternative* to being linked to other beliefs, and our Dogmatist is not obliged to choose between two bollards round which to tie his stern-rope. He may use both bollards. He may link his beliefs both to the world and to other beliefs.

There is room for a few more dialectical manoeuvres, room for a little more squirming. But I cannot see that in the end any remarks about 'links with the world' are likely to embarrass the infinite regressionist.

And on that note I leave infinite regression.

3

Reciprocity

The Stoics maintained that everything is fated, and they maintained that the art of divination exists. According to Diogenianus
(an Epicurean critic of Stoicism),

> Chrysippus has offered us a proof in which he tries to
> establish these contentions reciprocally (δι' ἀλλήλων). For he
> wants to show that everything happens in accordance with
> fate from the fact that divination exists; and he could not
> prove that divination exists unless he presupposed that
> everything occurs in accordance with fate. And what mode of
> proof could be more unsound (μοχθηρότερος) than this?
>
> (frag. 4 Gercke = Eusebius, *PE* IV iii 2–3)

Thus Chrysippus allegedly argued from P_1 to P_2, and then back
again from P_2 to P_1; and he allegedly offered these arguments as
proofs of P_1 and P_2. But his reasoning, according to the Epicurean
opponent, is reciprocal and therefore unsound.

Some critics accused Aristotle of committing a similar error in a
passage in the *Prior Analytics*. At *APr* 25a14–17 he offers a concise
proof of the convertibility of E-propositions, a proof, in other
words, that from 'No A is B' you may infer 'No B is A'. Then, at
25a20–2, he gives an argument for the convertibility of I-
propositions (from 'Some A is B' you may infer 'Some B is A')
which invokes the convertibility of E-propositions. Alexander of
Aphrodisias reports the following criticism.

> Some people think that in the proof ⟨of E-convertibility⟩ he
> assumes that I-propositions are convertible, and they accuse
> him of using reciprocal proof (ἡ δι' ἀλλήλων δεῖξις). For,
> wanting to show that E-propositions are convertible, he uses
> for this proof – so they say – I-propositions and their

58

convertibility; and a little later, showing the convertibility of I-propositions, he uses the convertibility of E-propositions. And this mode of proof is agreed to be unsound (μοχθήρος).

(*in APr* 31.27–32.3; cf. Philoponus, *in APr* 49.11–14)

Thus Aristotle, too, allegedly argued from P_1 to P_2 and then back again from P_2 to P_1; and he allegedly thought that he had thereby proved both P_1 and P_2.

In the two texts I have cited, we see Dogmatists snapping at Dogmatists. The charge of reciprocal reasoning is meant to show that the rival Dogmatist is mistaken, that his views are at best ungrounded. The sceptics, too, bring the charge of reciprocity against the Dogmatists. But they use the charge for specifically sceptical ends: reciprocity induces ἐποχή, suspension of judgement. Sextus refers explicitly some thirty-five times to the 'reciprocal mode of suspension (ὁ διάλληλος τρόπος τῆς ἐποχῆς)', the method of inducing scepticism by pointing to the impotence of reciprocal argument. Like Diogenianus, he characterizes reciprocal proof as 'most unsound (μοχθηρότατος)' (*M* III 99); and the reciprocal mode is correspondingly described as 'most perplexing (ἀπορώτατος)' (*M* VIII 445; IX 47; cf. VIII 379).

The reciprocal mode is the fifth of the Five Modes of Agrippa. Here is Sextus' formal account of it.

> The reciprocal mode comes about when what ought to be confirmatory of the matter in question requires warranty from the matter in question. Thus being unable to assume either matter for the establishment of the other, we suspend judgement about both. (*PH* I 169)

Diogenes Laertius gives the same description of the mode, and he adds an illustrative example:

> E.g. if someone wants to confirm that there are pores by the fact that there are effluences, and assumes this very fact to confirm that there are effluences. (IX 89)

A Sextan example: in the course of his attack on Aristotelian logic, Sextus considers the following sample syllogism:

> Socrates is a man
> No man is a quadruped
> Therefore, Socrates is not a quadruped

He comments on it as follows.

> They want to confirm the premiss 'No man is a quadruped'
> by induction from the particulars; and they wish to infer each
> of the particular propositions from 'No man is a quadruped'.
> Thus they fall into the perplexity of the reciprocal mode.
>
> (*PH* II 197)

Thus syllogisms – of this particular sort – cannot provide proofs. For they argue from a universal to a particular; and yet they must also invoke an argument from particular to universal. (This passage in Sextus is the origin of the notorious charge that syllogisms 'beg the question' if they are employed as proofs. A syllogism cannot *establish* that Socrates is not a quadruped; for we must already know that Socrates is not a quadruped in order to avail ourselves of the premiss that no man is a quadruped. I shall not comment on the merits of this argument.)

Sextus' example shows that we must interpret the notion of reciprocal proof a little more broadly than the other texts I have cited may have suggested. From those texts we might have inferred that reciprocity occurs when we are offered a pair of arguments ('P_2: so P_1'; 'P_1: so P_2') where the premiss of the first argument is the conclusion of the second argument, and *vice versa*. But in the Sextan example both arguments have several premisses. The first argument is a syllogism with *two* premisses ('No men are quadrupeds' and 'Socrates is a man'); the second argument is an induction with numerous premisses (of the form 'Socrates is a man and not a quadruped', 'Plato is a man and not a quadruped', 'Aristotle is a man and not a quadruped' . . .). So we cannot talk of *the* premiss of the argument.

Rather, we should explain reciprocity as follows. Reciprocity occurs when we are offered a pair of arguments 'A: so P_1' and 'B: so P_2', where P_2 is one of the premisses collected in A and P_1 is one of the premisses collected in B. More rigorously: let Π_1 and Π_2 be sets of propositions. Then the arguments 'Π_1: so P_1' and 'Π_2: so P_2' form a reciprocal pair just in case P_2 is a member of Π_1 and P_1 is a member of Π_2. Roughly: you argue reciprocally when you use the conclusion of one argument as a premiss in a second argument which itself is supposed to establish one of the premisses of the first argument.

Thus far I have talked only of *pairs* of arguments; and I shall in future restrict the term 'reciprocal' to cases in which exactly two arguments are involved. But it is plain that reciprocal arguments are a special case of a more general type of argumentation. For there is no need to restrict attention to pairs. We might think of three arguments, standing in the following relation to one another: 'P_3: so P_2'; 'P_2: so P_1'; 'P_1: so P_3'. Here there is what we might call circularity – you start with P_3 and end up at P_3 again. And the circles may be as large as you like. They may have four or five or six elements – or n elements for any n you like.

Since the arguments in the circle may each have several premisses, our account of circularity must accommodate the fact. We may have, say, 'A: so P_2', 'B: so P_1' 'C: so P_3', where P_2 is included in B, and P_1 is included in C, and P_3 is included in A. More rigorously: Let Π_1, Π_2, . . ., Π_n, be sets of propositions. Then the sequence of arguments 'Π_1: so P_1', 'Π_2: so P_2', . . ., 'Π_n: so P_n' is a circular argumentation just in case every P_i is included in Π_{i+1} (and P_n is included in Π_1). More informally: you argue in a circle when you produce a sequence of arguments such that the conclusion of one argument is a premiss for the next argument, and the conclusion of the last argument is a premiss for the first argument.

It is plain that reciprocity is a special case of circularity: reciprocal arguments are those circular arguments which have just two members. All reciprocal arguments are circular arguments, but not all circular arguments are reciprocal arguments.

I shall suppose that the 'reciprocity mode' is essentially an attack, not just upon reciprocal argument, but more generally upon circular argument. And I shall eventually discuss the credentials of the mode in the light of this supposition. But the supposition, though philosophically necessary (as I shall explain), is historically false – or over-simplified. So before I examine the mode as a general sceptical device, I shall say something about the way in which it actually functions in the writings of Sextus.

Sextus deploys the reciprocal mode, as I said, some thirty-five times. Several of these examples are – or seem to be – similar to the syllogistic example at *PH* II 197; and thus they are genuine illustrations of the type of argumentation which I have defined as reciprocal argument.[1] But more than half of Sextus' arguments are not of this type at all. Among these deviant cases, two groups may be distinguished.

An example of the first group is provided by the very first reference to the reciprocal mode in *PH* (the context is immaterial):

> If he judges the matter, he will of course say that he has judged it by a criterion – and for this criterion we shall seek a proof, and for the proof a criterion. For the proof will always require a criterion in order to be confirmed, and the criterion a proof in order to be shown to be true . . . And thus criterion and proof fall into the reciprocal mode. (*PH* I 116–17).

I am concerned – as usual – not with the soundness of Sextus' argument but with its form. And it is plain that it does not have the same form as those arguments which I have defined as reciprocal. For it does not consist of a *pair* of arguments, 'Π_1: so P_1', 'Π_2: so P_2', with P_1 in Π_2 and P_2 in Π_1.

Rather, we seem to be faced with an infinite regression of a special kind. The Dogmatist under attack is supposed to claim that K_1 is his criterion for judging that P_1. He then produces a putative proof, A_1, for the reliability of K_1; and next, a criterion, K_2, for the adequacy of A_1; and so on. Thus:

K_1: P_1 is true
A_1: K_1 is reliable
K_2: A_1 is sound
A_2: K_2 is reliable
K_3: A_2 is sound

.
.
.

There is no genuine reciprocity involved, since no proposition is ever *repeated*: the K_is are all different criteria, the A_is all different proofs.

We can, of course, see why Sextus invoked the notion of reciprocity here; for we do in fact oscillate from criteria to proofs and back again. There is, if you like, a *generic* reciprocity. But there is no *individual* reciprocity. A rough characterization of the group

---

1 See *PH* II 9, 36(?), 114(?), 196, 199, 202; *M* VIII 261(?), 342(?), 379/80; XI 183. (A question-mark indicates that it is not clear whether the case is of this type or not.)

to which this example belongs might run like this: we have generic reciprocity when we have an infinite sequence of claims, the even members of which fall into one epistemologically suspect class, and the odd members of which fall into another epistemologically suspect class. At *PH* I 116, the even members are of the form: 'A$_i$ is a proof that K$_i$ is reliable' – and all proofs are suspect and in need of support. The odd members are of the form 'K$_i$ is a criterion which ensures the soundness of A$_{i-1}$' – and all criteria are suspect and in need of support.

In many places where Sextus appeals to the reciprocal mode, it is an argument of this sort which he has in mind.[2] I shall say nothing here about the credentials of generic reciprocity; for, as far as I can see, it is properly construed as a special case of infinite regression, and I have already discussed infinite regressions.

As an illustration of the second group of deviant cases, take a passage from Sextus' discussion of the concept of cause:

> Now in order to conceive of a cause we must first recognize the effect, and in order to recognize the effect, as I said, we must first know the cause. Then the reciprocal mode of perplexity shows that both are inconceivable – we can form a conception neither of the cause as cause nor of the effect as effect. (*PH* III 22)

Here, too, there is no reciprocal argumentation of the sort I defined. Indeed, there is no argument at all. Rather, Sextus is concerned with reciprocal *conceptions* – or, better, with reciprocal *definitions*. For the Dogmatist is supposed to explain the concept of cause by saying

(C) A cause is what produces an effect,

and to explain the concept of effect by saying

(E) An effect is what is produced by a cause.

Now, so Sextus argues, (C) presupposes an understanding of the concept of effect, i.e. it presupposes (E). But (E) presupposes an understanding of the concept of cause, i.e. it presupposes (C).[3]

---

2 See *PH* I 172, 176, 186; II 68, 92/3, 183 (bis); III 35, 53; *M* VII 341; VIII 22, 29, 122, 181, 445(?).
3 On this see Jonathan Barnes, 'Ancient Skepticism and Causation', in M.F. Burnyeat (ed.), *The Skeptical Tradition* (Berkeley, 1983).

There are several examples of this sort of thing in Sextus.[4] I shall comment briefly on their substance later. Here I want only to insist that such examples are not pieces of reciprocal argument – for they are not pieces of argument at all. Again, we can see why Sextus should invoke the notion of reciprocity. But he cannot be invoking the particular notion of reciprocal argument.

Sextus thus calls upon the reciprocal mode in three distinct contexts: first, to deal with *genuinely* reciprocal arguments; secondly, to deal with *generically* reciprocating regressions; thirdly, to deal with reciprocal *definitions*. (There are some examples which it is hard to categorize with any confidence; and a few texts seem to convey no more than the vague thought that a Dogmatist is somehow obliged by his theory both to do A before he does B and also to do B before he does A.) Sextus never explicitly marks any difference among the three sorts of case; and in a loose sense he can reasonably say that all of them involve reciprocity – in each type of case, the Dogmatist goes from A to B and back to A again. But the cases *are* distinct, and they need to be distinguished. Indeed, they need to be distinguished by the Pyrrhonist; for they raise quite different problems.

There is another curious fact about Sextus' use of the reciprocal mode. All the cases he considers are cases of reciprocity. All, that is to say, involve *pairs* of arguments (or of generic types or of definitions). He nowhere examines or criticizes a circular argument with more than two elements, a circular argument which is not also reciprocal. How is this fact to be explained? We shall hardly entertain the thought that Sextus might have had no objection to large circles, holding that reciprocal argument was the only unsound form of circular argument. Indeed, we must surely suppose that his objections to reciprocity were intended to hold generally against *all* circular reasoning, for otherwise he would have left a loophole for Dogmatic belief. (I mean that the Dogmatists could produce circles containing three or more elements, and thus escape Sextus' objections to reciprocity. And that would be ridiculous.)

---

4 See *PH* III 242; *M* VII 426; VIII 86; IX 47; *M* III 99. In the first three of these passages Sextus' example is the same – an alleged reciprocity in the Stoic definition of φαντασία καταληπτική.

Aristotle discusses circular proof in the chapter of the *Posterior Analytics* to which I referred in the previous chapter. He shows himself explicitly aware of the fact that circular reasoning may contain any number of component arguments. But he chooses to discuss only the simplest case, i.e. the reciprocal case.

> For it makes no difference whether they say that it bends back through many items or through few, nor whether through few or through two.   (*APst* 72b36–7)

Large circles or small, many items or few – it is all the same. The objection to circularity does not depend on the magnitude of the circle. I suppose that this Aristotelian thought lies behind Sextus' procedure. (Later I shall suggest that the Aristotelian chapter may actually have inspired Agrippa to collect his modes.) In Sextus' text we find only reciprocal arguments. But the explanation is, as it were, pedagogical: reciprocal arguments are the simplest sort of circular reasoning, and since no extra issues are raised by larger circles, the exposition may properly restrict itself to reciprocity. Whether or not this is *true* – whether or not large circles are no different, in any epistemologically important features, from small circles – is an issue to which I shall return.

In the last chapter, I asked why infinite regression should be thought to lead to ἐποχή. The same question arises in the case of reciprocity. Since the answer in this case is parallel to the answer in the regressive case, I shall be brief.

Clearly the fact – if it is a fact – that Chrysippus argued reciprocally for the existence of fate is no reason at all for us to suspend judgement over the existence of fate. For even if reciprocal arguments are bad arguments, the fact that Chrysippus argued badly for the existence of fate does not imply that there are no *good* reasons for admitting (or for denying) the existence of fate.

Again, we must understand a qualifying phrase: 'as far as this argument goes', ὅσον ἐπὶ τούτῳ. As far as Chrysippus' argument goes, we must suspend judgement. If the *only* reason we have for accepting or rejecting the existence of fate is supplied by Chrysippus' reasoning, then we should suspend judgement. And why? Because reciprocal arguments are *bad* arguments; and if the only reason we have for accepting or rejecting P is a bad argument, then we should neither accept nor reject P but suspend judgement.

It might be said, and truly, that the ὅσον ἐπὶ τούτῳ qualification leaves the reciprocal mode with little to do; for surely it will hardly *ever* be the case that the *only* reason we have for accepting or rejecting P is a reciprocal argument. (The same, as I observed, holds of the regressive mode: it will hardly ever be true that the *only* reason we have for accepting or rejecting P is an infinite sequence of arguments.) This is surely true; but it does not mean that the reciprocal mode lacks real interest. For if the mode will rarely, if ever, be useful by itself, it may still have power as a member of a set or team of modes. And in my last chapter I shall try to show that as a team-member it is powerful, even if as an individual performer it lacks strength.

Now the chief question is this: What, if anything, is actually wrong with circular reasoning? But before I turn to this question, it may be diverting to record that some ancient thinkers actually *defended* circular argument. Three texts, or groups of texts, are relevant.

The first group clusters about Porphyry's *Isagoge* or *Introduction to Philosophy*. In a notorious passage, Porphyry explains that a genus is something which stands over species and that a species is something which is included in a genus (*isag* 4.4–9); and 'in saying this', as his commentator Ammonius remarks, 'Porphyry is rightly thought to have used reciprocal proof' (*in Porph isag* 74.8–10). After a brief discussion, Ammonius concludes that Porphyry's procedure is in fact unobjectionable; for genus and species are correlatives, and

> relatives (τὰ πρός τι) subsist at the same time and are thought of at the same time as one another . . . Thus it is absolutely necessary that anyone who is expounding one of them should refer to the other; for if you are ignorant of one relative, you will not know the other either.   (*in Porph isag* 76.5–10)

No doubt Ammonius is right; but his remarks seem a little *ad hoc.*

A later commentator, Elias, is more satisfactory; and I quote an extract from his discussion of the same passage in Porphyry:

> But, they say, we have fallen unawares into reciprocal proof, a thing which philosophers should avoid. For in describing

the genus, we referred to the species, and in describing the species we referred to the genus. We reply that reciprocal proof is not always to be avoided. For if the objects with which the accounts (λόγοι) are concerned do not depend for their subsistence upon one another (like cows and horses and so on), then we should avoid reciprocal proof with all our power. But if the objects do depend for their existence upon one another, then it is not possible to give an account of them except by reciprocal proof. For just as it is impossible for a shadow to be still while the object which casts it is not still, so it is impossible for the accounts not to require one another when the objects with which the accounts are concerned do require one another.   (*in Porph isag* 62.9–19)[5]

Since correlatives are indissolubly linked to one another, their definitions or λόγοι may – indeed must – also be interlinked or reciprocal.

What exactly is Elias defending? Although he talks of 'reciprocal proof', he is plainly not defending what I have called *genuine* reciprocity. Elsewhere, indeed, he insists that reciprocal argument must be avoided in *all* ἀποδείξεις or proofs (*proleg* 9.23–5). Nor is he defending *generic* reciprocity; for the text of Porphyry on which he is commenting does not contain a generically reciprocal or regressive argument – indeed, it does not contain any argument at all. Despite his reference to 'reciprocal proof', it is clear that Elias is actually concerned with reciprocal *definition*. (In fact, he distinguishes, in a thoroughly traditional fashion, between ὁρισμοί or 'real' definitions and ὑπογραφαί or outline descriptions; and he holds that reciprocity is never legitimate for ὁρισμοί but only for ὑπογραφαί (*in Porph isag* 58.20–8). But the distinction need not trouble us here, and I shall continue to speak simply of definitions.)

In sum, Elias holds that when you are defining relative terms, then your definitions may – or rather, must – be reciprocal. This may seem a modest enough position. Even so, if Elias is right, some of Sextus' applications of the reciprocal mode will be in error. In particular, cause and effect are correlatives, in Elias' sense; hence, according to Elias, reciprocal definition is permissible – indeed obligatory – in their case.

5 See also Olympiodorus, *in Cat* 109.21–8; David, *in Porph isag* 132.6–25, 144.26–31.

But is Elias' modest suggestion right? I do not think so. First, it is perfectly possible to define causes without referring to effects, and *vice versa*. Sextus offered us the formulae:

(C) A cause is what produces an effect,

and

(E) An effect is what is produced by a cause.

We need only make a trivial modification to these formulae to get:

(C*) A thing is a cause if it brings something about,

and

(E*) A thing is an effect if it is brought about by something.

Here (C*) does not use the word 'effect' and (E*) does not use the word 'cause', and so there is no reciprocity. But – and secondly – no doubt (C*) and (E*) seem far too thin and weak to function as definitions; and no doubt, too, what we really want is a definition or an explanation of the causal *relation*, i.e. we want an analytical definition of the form

(CR) x causes y $=_{df}$ P

Now if we produce something of the form (CR), must we thereby refer to effects? Clearly not. Various thinkers have made various attempts to produce satisfactory definitions of causation in the form of (CR). None of them does, and none of them need, make explicit reference to effects.

Yet there is a little more to be said. Plainly, x causes y if and only if y is caused by x, i.e. if and only if y is an effect of x. Thus, given (CR), we can at once produce

(ER) y is effected by x $=_{df}$ P

So (ER) is, in a sense, indissolubly linked with (CR). You cannot define causes without implicitly defining effects, and you cannot define effects without implicitly defining causes. If Elias was groping for this point, then it was a truth he was groping for. But the truth has nothing to do with reciprocal definition, as I have explained the notion, and we should not talk of reciprocity here at all. For (ER) and (CR) do not define two different notions in terms of one another; rather, they define one and the same notion, the notion of the causal relation.

Thus when Elias says that, in the case of correlatives, reciprocal definitions are unavoidable, he is wrong – or at best he is speaking in a highly misleading way. And the best defence of Porphyry's controversial procedure over genus and species will not invoke the sort of reciprocity to which Sextus objects.

The Porphyrian case apart, we might still wonder if reciprocal definitions are ever permissible. The answer to this question depends on what we expect from a definition. If the function of a definition is to introduce or explain a new term by way of terms already understood, then reciprocity must in all cases be avoided. For suppose that (C) – 'A cause is what produces an effect' – defines the 'new' term 'cause' by means of words already understood. Then (E) – 'An effect is what is produced by a cause' – is at best superfluous and at worst misconceived. For 'effect', the term which (E) purportedly defines or introduces for the first time, is – by hypothesis – a term already known and understood.

Now though definitions sometimes serve to introduce and establish new terms, they do not always function in this fashion. And so the argument I have just sketched does not show that reciprocal definitions are always improper. But I shall not pursue this issue any further, since it is tangential to the main sceptical circle.

So much for Porphyry and his commentators. My second group of reciprocal defenders clusters about the rhetorician Hermogenes, who was a contemporary of Galen. There is a connexion between this group and the Porphyrian group. In one of his works, Hermogenes appears to indulge in something like reciprocal definition; for he says that 'pretty well all stylistic features are discovered and become plain reciprocally' (*id* I iii [= *Rhetores Graeci* II 279 Spengel]). Later commentators defended him: they insisted that reciprocal definition is permissible in the case of relatives – and one of them expressly appealed to the example of Porphyry on genus and species.[6]

But there is a second and more interesting reference to recip-

6 John Doxapatres refers to Porphyry: see his scholia to Hermogenes, in *Rhetores Graeci* [*Rhet Gr*] VI 160–1 Walz; cf. Maximus Planudes, in *Rhet Gr* V 470 Walz; anon., in *Rhet Gr* VII.2 928n69 Walz.

rocity in Hermogenes. In the account of 'conjectural inference' or στοχασμός in his book on *Issues*, Hermogenes distinguishes a form which he calls 'co-established inference (στοχασμός συγκατασκευαζόμενος)'. He explains it thus:

> A co-established inference is made when the signs of the matter are established reciprocally (δι' ἀλλήλων). E.g. the prisoners had to be freed at the festival of Thesmophoria. A man suspected his servant of adultery with his wife. He imprisoned the servant and left town. His wife freed the man at the Thesmophoria while her husband was still away. The servant ran off. The husband returned and was found murdered. Then the wife was accused of conspiracy. Now the fact that the husband was killed by the servant is established by way of the adultery, and the fact of the adultery is established by way of the killing. And in general, they are established reciprocally – but together with other facts, of course (the man's suspicion, the wife's freeing the servant, and so on).
>
> (*stas* III [= *Rhet Gr* II 152 Spengel])

This is evidently an example of genuine reciprocity. We are invited to conclude, first, from the evidence of the adultery that the servant killed his master, and secondly, from the evidence of the murder that the slave committed adultery. (Thus we have two signs or pieces of evidence that the wife is guilty of conspiracy, and each sign is established through the other.) Hermogenes expressly notes, in the last sentence of the extract, that other premises are involved. In short, we have, according to Hermogenes, a pair of arguments of the form

$$A_1, A_2, \ldots, A_n, P_2: \text{ so } P_1$$
$$B_1, B_2, \ldots, B_m, P_1: \text{ so } P_2$$

and that is the very form of a genuinely reciprocal argumentation.

Hermogenes appears to assume that there is nothing wrong with these 'co-established inferences'. His commentators were embarrassed: the passage caused much discussion and controversy, and in the end Hermogenes found no defenders. I cite one late text.

> Here Hermogenes says that unclear items – the murder and the adultery – are proved reciprocally. He is wrong. For this sort of proof is contrary to reason. In every inference, the test

of what is unclear and in need of judgement depends on some evident sign; and the evident signs here are the suspicion of adultery – *not* the adultery itself – and the freeing of the servant. It is through these that it is established that the master was killed by the servant, and by way of the murder we establish not the suspicion of adultery (there is no need to establish what is evident) but the adultery itself. Hence there is no genuine case of reciprocal proof.

(Maximus Planudes, in *Rhet Gr* V 297 Walz)[7]

Thus Planudes maintains that reciprocal proof – genuine reciprocal proof – is contrary to reason; and he supposes that Hermogenes has given a faulty analysis of the imaginary court case which he describes.

Planudes does not explain why reciprocal proof is wrong any more than Hermogenes indicates why he sees no objection to it. But he does give an illustration which invites a brief digression.

> Suppose that you do not know where Dio or Theo lives but that you do know where Plato lives. Someone says to you: 'Dio lives where Theo lives, and Theo lives where Dio lives.' Now if he goes no further and stops there, the proof is reciprocal. But if he adds that Dio or Theo lives where Plato lives, then there is a clear proof of the statement.
>
> (Maximus Planudes, in *Rhet Gr* V 295–6 Walz)

The example is found elsewhere.[8] The dummy names 'Theo' and 'Dio' suggest a Stoic origin; and an anonymous text apparently confirms the suggestion.

> How will an enquiry of this sort come to an end if the elements of each proof are reciprocally generated? For such things will remain controverted. Thus there is an argument which the Stoics call reciprocal, and which is ἀναπόδεικτος. E.g. Dio lives where Theo lives; and Theo lives where Dio lives. Such an argument, which, as I say, offers a reciprocal

---

7 See also Sopater, in *Rhet Gr* IV 460–1 Walz; Marcellinus, ibid. 461–3; anon., ibid. 463; Epiphanius, ibid. 465; anon., *Rhet Gr* VII.1 381–9 Walz. (The last text is the most elaborate; but it adds little of substance to the slimmer commentaries.)
8 See anon., in *Rhet Gr* VII.2 928n69 Walz; Elias, *proleg* 9.12–21.

proof,⁹ is ἀναπόδεικτος and never comes to a conclusion. And the same occurs, they say, with co-established inferences.

(anon., in Rhet Gr VII.1 383 Walz)

This passage undeniably shows that some Stoics had spoken of reciprocal argument. But the text as a whole has been misunderstood.

It has been inferred that the Stoics reflected on the rhetoricians' idea of co-established inference, that they defended a variety of reciprocal proof (holding it to be ἀναπόδεικτος or indemonstrable), and that the sceptical mode of reciprocity was directed against – or influenced by – this Stoic view. Were these inferences warranted, we should have in the anonymous scholiast on Hermogenes an important and intriguing witness to the history of reciprocal argument.

But the inferences are not warranted. First, there is no evidence that the Stoics knew the rhetoricians' co-established inferences: the 'they' in the last sentence of my extract refers not to the Stoics but to the earlier critics of Hermogenes whom our anonymous scholiast is reviewing. The scholiast does not state or imply that any Stoics actually referred to co-established inferences.

Secondly, there is no evidence that the Stoics defended what they called reciprocal arguments. In Stoic terminology, the word ἀναπόδεικτος does indeed mean 'indemonstrable', and it is applied to fundamental – and fundamentally *valid* – argument-forms. But our scholiast uses the word in a different sense: he regularly uses ἀναπόδεικτος in the sense of 'non-probative'. Thus the text does not say that reciprocal argument is indemonstrable, and therefore fundamentally valid. It says that it is non-probative. Moreover, the phrase 'and which is non-probative' expresses the scholiast's own view and not a view which he ascribes to the Stoics. Perhaps the Stoics did regard reciprocal argument as non-probative. The text does not say that they did.

The text is interesting and frustrating. It allows us to say that some Stoics had discussed – or at least had named – reciprocal argument. It tempts us to guess that they, like other ancient logicians, had rejected it as non-probative. But we cannot tell

---

9 Reading ὁ διάλληλόν [διάλληλός Walz] φημι τὴν ἀπόδειξιν ἔχων, with von Arnim: see VII.1 384.7–8 Walz. (But note that von Arnim's text at SVF II 273 is horribly mutilated.)

which Stoics were interested in the thing. We do not know what or how much they said about it. We cannot even be sure exactly what sort of argument they took to be reciprocal. (For our texts present the example of Dio and Theo in telegrammatic form, and several different interpretations can be ventured.)

After this journey through relatively remote texts, I return for my final group of defenders of reciprocity to a familiar author and a familiar work. In the *Posterior Analytics* Aristotle observes that

> some hold that knowledge can only come from proof. But they maintain that nothing prevents there from being a proof of everything – for it is possible for proof to be circular and reciprocal. (*APst* 72b15–18)

Aristotle adverts to defenders of genuinely reciprocal argumentation, and we must believe that in Aristotle's day some thinkers had expressly allowed the legitimacy of circular proof. But although Aristotle argues against their view at some length (*APst* 72b25–73a20), he does not tell us who his opponents were; he does not explain under what conditions they accepted circularity; and he does not indicate how – if at all – they argued in defence of the sorts of proofs they accepted. Aristotle's reticence is frustrating. Scholarly conjectures on the matter have taught us little.[10]

Thus little, alas, emerges from the meagre texts in defence of reciprocity. A few ancient thinkers did indeed accept reciprocal or circular argumentation. But we do not know exactly what kind of argument they sanctioned, and we do not know what (if anything) they alleged in its defence. What, next, can be said against it? Why is circular reasoning a bad thing, 'to be avoided by the philosophers'?

Once or twice Sextus suggests that with circular reasoning, as with infinite regressions, we have no starting-point (*PH* III 22; cf. II 9). But, again, the remark is implausible: why not start wherever you like? Any point on a circle – as Heraclitus observed – is a starting-point.

---

10 Nevertheless, I may be allowed to refer to Jonathan Barnes, 'Aristotle, Menaechmus, and Circular Proof', *Classical Quarterly* 26, 1976, 278–92.

Reciprocity

Once Sextus connects reciprocal argumentation with trying to prove 'the unknown by way of the unknown' (*M* VIII 86), and hence with a class of mistakes – or supposed mistakes – which are generally collected under the title of *obscurum per obscurius*, proving the obscure by way of the more obscure.[11] The connexion between reciprocity and *obscurum per obscurius* points to an objection which Sextus often brings – at least implicitly – against reciprocity. The objection involves the notion of priority. Here is a simple case:

> Thus the reciprocal mode turns up, according to which the mind must *first* have been judged (προκεκρίσθαι) if the senses are to be decided, and the senses must *first* be determined (προδιακρίνεσθαι) if the mind is to be assessed. (*PH* II 68)

You must judge the mind *before* you judge the senses, and also judge the senses *before* you judge the mind.[12] In general, reciprocal proof requires you to do A before B and also to do B before A. And that is evidently absurd.

Now Sextus is surely right to imply that you cannot *both* do A before B *and* do B before A. But why does he think that this is an objection to reciprocal proof? He imagines, I suppose, that if you prove that P_1 by way of an argument 'P_2: so P_1,', then you come to believe P_1 on the basis of an antecedent belief in P_2. Hence you must *first* believe P_2 (without yet believing P_1), and *then* acquire the belief that P_1. Thus Sextus construes proofs as psychological events, which occupy a period of time and which end with the production of a new belief (or perhaps of a new item of knowledge). Suppose that Chrysippus simultaneously comes up with two proofs: 'Divination is possible: so all is fated'; 'All is fated: so divination is possible.' Then in virtue of the first proof, he must have believed that divination was possible *before* he came to believe that all was fated; and in virtue of the second proof, he must have believed that

---

11 See further Karel Janáček, *Sextus Empiricus' Sceptical Methods* (Prague, 1972), pp.35–7.
12 For the priority objection see *PH* II 9, 199, 202; III 22; *M* VII 426; VIII 122, 181, 261; *M* III 99 (priority expressed by way of verbs with the prefix προ-); *PH* II 9; *M* VIII 342, 380 (the preposition πρό); *PH* II 20 (the adverb πρότερον); *PH* I 117; *M* VII 341, 426; VIII 261 (the verb περιμένειν).

all was fated *before* he came to believe that divination was possible. And that is absurd.

Sextus' argument has a shine to it. An ingenious caviller might, it is true, seek to defend Chrysippus' putative procedure along the following lines. Suppose that Chrysippus already believes P_2. Then at noon, say, he proves P_1 from P_2, thereby acquiring the belief that P_1. But he at once *forgets* P_2. Why may he not now, at 12.15, proceed to prove P_2 from P_1? In general, given sufficiently bizarre conditions on his memory, Chrysippus may happily, and without contradiction, go on forever proving first P_1 from P_2 and then P_2 from P_1. But whatever we make of such fantasies, they are not worth pursuing here; for evidently they do not touch the nerve of Sextus' argument.

The real difficulty with the argument is this. It supposes that proofs are essentially ways of forming or generating beliefs. It works against the Dogmatists only insofar as they appeal to proofs in order to give an account of how our beliefs may be formed or generated. But the Dogmatists were not – or should not have been – concerned solely or primarily with this. Rather, they were – or should have been – concerned with the warranty or justification of beliefs. Now it is plain that I may be justified in believing that P_1 because I believe that P_2 even if I originally *acquired* the belief that P_2 after I had acquired the belief that P_1. Something like this is true, I suppose, of very many of our actual beliefs. I am pretty sure that I myself believed the *Magna Moralia* to be spurious some years before I acquired the beliefs which now warrant my confidence that it is spurious. The beliefs which once led to or generated my belief in the spuriousness of the *Magna Moralia* must have antedated that belief; the beliefs which now warrant or justify it did not – and that is no objection to them. For justification is not a matter of producing new beliefs but of warranting old ones. The fact that reciprocal proofs cannot be used to generate fresh beliefs does not show that they cannot be used to warrant existing beliefs.

Thus Sextus' standard – if implicit – objection to reciprocal proof is an *ignoratio elenchi*. Or at least, it is an *ignoratio elenchi* if, as I have supposed, the priority which it invokes is a temporal or chronological priority. But temporal priority is not the only variety of priority. Aristotle's main objection to circular proof also turns on the notion of priority but not on the notion of temporal priority. According to Aristotle,

> it is clear that it is impossible to prove anything circularly if a proof must depend on what is prior and more familiar. For it is impossible for the same things at the same time to be prior and posterior to the same things. (*APst* 72b25–8)

It is quite clear from the context that 'prior' and 'posterior' do not here refer to temporal relations: Aristotle's objection to circular reasoning does not turn on any ideas about the order in which our beliefs are acquired.

The Aristotelian thought is echoed by numerous later writers. Thus Ammonius:

> in proofs of this sort the same things are assumed to be both prior and posterior to, both more clear and more unclear than, the same things. (*in Porph isag* 75.13–15)

And Elias:

> Reciprocal proof should be avoided by philosophers; for it makes the same things prior and posterior to, more clear and more unclear than, explanatory of and explained by, the same things. For when we prove by way of Dio where Theo lives, Dio is clearer, prior and explanatory. And when, on the contrary, the proof is by way of Theo, Theo is clearer, prior and explanatory.
> (*proleg* 9.15–20; cf. David, *proleg* 25.4–15)

Priority here is not a temporal but an 'epistemic' property – it is a property of the same sort as clarity and explanatoriness.

The general thrust of the Aristotelian objection to circularity and reciprocity is this. If 'Π: so P' is a proof of P, then there must be certain epistemic relations holding between the members of Π and P: the members of Π must together *ground* or support P; they must *explain* P or make P intelligible or rational to believe; they must *illuminate* P; and so on. (These relations are different from and additional to any logical relations which link Π and P. In Aristotle's view, Π must entail P if 'Π: so P' is to be a proof or ἀπόδειξις. For a proof is a sort of syllogism: it is a deductively valid argument. But the logical relations, in virtue of which 'Π: so P' is a valid argument, are distinct from the *epistemic* relations which make 'Π: so P' a proof and on which the Aristotelian objection to circular proof turns.)

Let us sum this up by saying that if 'Π: so P' is a proof, then each member of Π must be *epistemically prior* to P. Now Aristotle plainly takes the relation of epistemic priority to have two salient features: he takes it to be asymmetrical, and he takes it to be transitive. In other words, if X is prior to Y, then it follows that Y is *not* prior to X (this is asymmetry). And if X is prior to Y and Y is prior to Z, then X is prior to Z (this is transitivity).

Suppose, then, that we are offered a reciprocal argumentation, say the pair of arguments: 'Π$_1$: so P$_1$'; 'Π$_2$: so P$_2$'. Now if the first argument is a proof, then each member of Π$_1$ is prior to P$_1$. And since P$_2$ is in Π$_1$, P$_2$ is prior to P$_1$. But then, by asymmetry, P$_1$ is *not* prior to P$_2$. Hence not all the members of Π$_2$ are prior to P$_2$. Hence 'P$_1$: so P$_2$' cannot be a proof. It follows that any reciprocal argumentation contains at most *one* argument which is a proof. Hence reciprocal argumentation is not probative, i.e. the pair of arguments cannot prove both P$_1$ and P$_2$. Asymmetry alone is thus enough to kill off reciprocal proof.

Circular proof is tougher, and must be attacked by a combination of asymmetry and transitivity. Consider the very simplest sort of circle, consisting of three single-premissed arguments: 'P$_3$: so P$_2$'; 'P$_2$: so P$_1$'; 'P$_1$: so P$_3$'. Each constituent of this circle is supposed to be a proof; so P$_3$ will be prior to P$_2$, P$_2$ to P$_1$ and P$_1$ to P$_3$. Then by transitivity, P$_3$ is prior to P$_1$. But by asymmetry, P$_3$ is not prior to P$_1$. Hence at least one item in the circle is not a proof. Hence the circle is non-probative.

This argument must be generalized in two ways: it must be extended to cover circles of any size, and it must be extended to embrace arguments with more than one premiss. But it should be easy to see how these generalizations can be made. And it should be clear that asymmetry and transitivity will together scupper circular argumentation.

The question, then, is this: Is the relation of epistemic priority asymmetrical and transitive? If it is, then the sceptic has made out his case against circular and reciprocal proof.

It might be thought that it is simply *obvious* that epistemic priority is both asymmetrical and transitive. After all, if X is prior to Y, then surely Y can not be prior to X? And if X is prior to Y and Y is prior to Z, then surely it follows at once that X is prior to Z? But we need to remember that our talk of epistemic 'priority' is metaphorical – or at any rate, that it does not invoke the normal temporal notion of priority. Although in the literal sense the word 'prior' picks out a relation which is asymmetrical and transitive, we cannot infer that the word picks out a similar relation in its transferred use. More generally, we use a variety of metaphors in speaking of epistemic relations ('grounding' and 'supporting' are two familiar examples); and the terms we use often seem 'evidently' to pick out a relation of a particular sort. But this may be a specious evidence – we may find ourselves seduced to our intellectual ruin by the paint and powder of a raddled metaphor.

It might be thought, secondly, that at least one of the terms used in the Aristotelian account of epistemic priority is employed in a non-transferred sense, and that here asymmetry (surely) and transitivity (perhaps) may quickly be established. The term I mean is 'explanatory'. If X is explanatory of Y, then surely Y is not explanatory of X? And, perhaps less evidently, if X explains Y and Y explains Z, then surely X ('at one remove') explains Z? Since Aristotle invokes literal and not metaphorical explanatoriness, there is no danger of specious evidence here.

True – but then it is far from clear that the notion of explanatoriness must be a constituent of the notion of epistemic priority. In the *Posterior Analytics* Aristotle is concerned with a very special type of proof or argument, a type which he calls ἀπόδειξις and which he regards as the paradigm of scientific argumentation. In a scientific proof or ἀπόδειξις, Aristotle maintains, the premisses must be explanatory of the conclusion. But Aristotle does not hold that the same condition governs the premisses of *any* justificatory argument; and we should not ourselves try to extend the scope of Aristotle's thesis.

For it seems clear, first, that the premisses of a *proof* need not in all cases explain the conclusion. Thus according to Proclus,

> many people have held that geometry does not consider explanations and the question 'Why?'. Amphinomus held this view.　　　　　　　　　　　　　　(*in Eucl* 202.9–11)

Amphinomus, a contemporary of Aristotle, must evidently have thought that in geometrical proofs the premisses are not explanatory, even though geometrical proofs are surely paradigmatic proofs, proofs in the strictest sense of the term.

Secondly, in everyday arguments the premisses are not usually explanatory of the conclusion. Rather, they stand as evidence or signs of its truth. Hermogenes' fictitious orator concluded that the servant had committed adultery with the wife, and he concluded this from the fact that the servant had killed the husband. The orator did not, of course, suppose that the murder explained the adultery. The murder was cited as evidence – perhaps even as conclusive evidence – for the adultery. It was, in the ancient jargon, a sign and not a cause. (And Hermogenes explicitly talks of signs, not of causes.)

Thus even if Aristotle's appeal to explanatoriness will suffice to exclude circular ἀποδείξεις, it will not exclude all circular proofs, let alone all circular arguments.

It is plain that we need a clearer understanding of epistemic priority before we can proceed any further. What exactly *is* epistemic priority? Unless we can answer this question, we cannot sensibly ask what properties the relation has. So what should we say? Well, although the notion of epistemic priority was introduced in connexion with Aristotelian proofs, we are not here specifically interested in ἀποδείξεις. For reciprocity and circularity may infect any sort of proof or argument and are not proper to scientific demonstrations; and, in the context of scepticism, we must be interested in any argument in which the premisses are – or are alleged to be – sufficient to warrant belief in the conclusion. In short, we are centrally concerned with the notion of warranty or justification. The relation which matters in the present context is the relation which holds between two propositions when – very roughly speaking – the one justifies you in holding the other.

This relation is in a further sense relative – it is concerned not with what warrants beliefs *simpliciter* but with what warrants *your* beliefs or *my* beliefs. The notion is thus distinct from what might be called an 'objective' notion of justification, a notion in which epistemologists have also been interested. I mention this fact in order to be able to push aside a tempting but irrelevant argument. The modern literature has stock examples which are designed to show that 'objective' justification is not a transitive relation. Here is one of them.[13] Consider the following three propositions.

> P_3: There were two consuls at Rome
> P_2: There was a prime number of consuls at Rome
> P_1: There was an odd number of consuls at Rome

Now – the suggestion is – P_3 plainly warrants P_2; for P_2 actually follows from P_3, and if there were two consuls then there certainly was a prime number of consuls. Equally, but in a different way, P_2 warrants P_1; for of the infinity of prime numbers, all but one are odd, so that if there is a prime number of anything, then it is overwhelmingly probable that there is an odd number of it. But of course P_3 cannot warrant P_1 – that there are two things is hardly a warrant that there is an odd number of things. On the contrary, P_3 warrants the contradictory of P_1; for P_3 entails not-P_1. Thus the sort of justification or warranty illustrated by this example is not transitive: P_3 warrants P_2 and P_2 warrants P_1; but P_3 does not warrant P_1.

This is ingenious and no doubt important. But I do not think that it is directly relevant to my present concerns. I do not think it proves that justification, in the sense which matters here, is not transitive. For even if it is true that, in the example, P_2 in some objective sense warrants P_1, it does not seem to me to be true that if I believe P_2 I am *thereby* justified in believing P_1. Whether or not my belief in P_2 justifies a belief in P_1 depends, *inter alia*, on my other beliefs. In particular, if I also believe P_3 – and especially if my belief in P_2 is justified by a belief in P_3 – then belief in P_2 does not justify belief in P_1.

So the epistemic priority we are looking for must be 'subjective' or relative to a given system of beliefs. A first, rough attempt to explain it, then, might look like this:

> X is epistemically prior to Y in my belief system just in case I
> am justified in believing Y because I believe X.

13 John Watkins drew my attention to the example. See further his *Science and Scepticism* (Princeton, 1984), pp.61–4.

X, or rather my belief in X, provides me with my warrant for believing in Y. (It might be different in your belief system: your belief in Y might be what justified you in believing X. For example, the wife may justifiably believe that the servant killed her husband because she knows that he has committed adultery with her. But a suspicion of adultery may not be what warrants the husband's belief that it is the servant who poisoned his food. Rather, he might finally believe in his wife's infidelity when he hears the servant chucklingly confess that the mushrooms he dished up for dinner were death-caps.)

The first attempt will not quite do. For X may be one of a whole set of reasons which together warrant my belief in Y. (I may argue to Y not from a single premiss, the premiss that X holds, but from a set of propositions one of which is X.) Hence we need to accommodate the case in which X is just one of the things on which my belief in Y depends. We might try this:

> X is epistemically prior to Y in my belief system just in case I am justified in believing Y because of a set of beliefs, one of which is my belief in X.

And we may as well put this a little more rigorously, thus:

> P_2 is epistemically prior to P_1 for believer x just in case P_2 is a member of a set of propositions Π_1, and x is justified in believing that P_1 because x believes the members of Π_1.

I doubt if this formulation is exactly right. But I am fairly sure that it is not wildly wrong – and I hope it will be good enough for the moment.

Then is this relation of epistemic priority asymmetrical and transitive? If P_2 is one of a set of beliefs which justifies my belief that P_1, does it follow that P_1 cannot be a member of a set of beliefs which justifies my belief that P_2? I hope you may agree that it is at least not *obvious* that the answer to this question is Yes – that it is at least not *obvious* that epistemic priority is asymmetrical. And the same holds, and more so, for transitivity. If P_3 belongs to a set of beliefs which justifies P_2 and P_2 belongs to a set of beliefs which justifies P_1, does it follow that P_3 belongs to a set of beliefs which justifies P_1? Again, it is not obvious – it is not obvious to me – that this is so.

I think there are two reasons why we are tempted to take it as obvious that epistemic priority is asymmetrical and transitive. First, we are seduced – as I have said before – by the metaphor of priority, and we tacitly ascribe to epistemic priority those properties which evidently hold of temporal priority. Secondly, and no less importantly, we tend to think in terms of the simplest examples. If we look at the simple Chrysippean reciprocity, it is difficult not to be sure that there is something badly wrong with reciprocal argument. But it does not follow, and we should resist the temptation to infer, that the Chrysippean reciprocity is unacceptable precisely because epistemic priority is asymmetrical and transitive; and hence we should not conclude from this example that there is something wrong with every reciprocity and with every circle. Most cases are complex cases, and complex cases are unlikely to be clear cases.

But if the properties of epistemic priority are not obvious, how can we establish them by argument? I am not sure. I shall end this chapter with two inconclusive lines of thought. The first proposes an analogy or model which is intended to make non-transitive justification seem somehow attractive and plausible. The second offers a popular argument which purports to show that the analogy or model is misleading and that circular argumentation cannot ever be satisfactory.

First, the analogy. You have a vast collection of flag-poles and flags. There are thousands – indeed millions – of them. You plant the poles all over the surface of the earth. They need not be planted at regular intervals: they may come in clumps and clusters, there may be forests of flag-poles and there may be relatively desert places. But no flag may be more than a few miles from its nearest neighbour, and most flags will have several flags within a mile of them. In addition to the flags and the flag-poles, you have a stock of ropes, an extraordinarily large stock. The ropes come in various lengths. The shortest rope is about a mile long, the longest rope is several hundred miles long. You must tie the flag-poles together. The tying and the planting may be carried out concurrently; but the order in which you plant the poles need not at all determine the way in which you rope them together, and the way the poles are roped together will not reveal the order in which they were originally planted.

The flags are all numbered. The ropes have a 'direction' in the sense that their ends are differently coloured: one end of every rope is green, the other is red. There are a few rules which determine how you may rope the poles together. The first rule is that every pole must have at least one green end attached to it. A second rule is permissive: a pole may have any number of ropes tied to it. A third rule says that at most one rope may directly link two poles – you may not tie one pole to another by several strands of rope. A fourth rule requires – trivially – that no flag-pole ever be roped to itself. It is also true that no flag-pole is directly roped to any pole which is more than a few hundred miles away from it; this is not, however, a rule – it is contingently determined by the fact that no rope is more than a few hundred miles long.

When your task is finished, the surface of the earth will be criss-crossed by ropes. The criss-crossing will construct a large net or web. At the nodes or knots of the web there are the numbered flags, waving in the winds.

The rules do not determine any particular configuration or type of configuration for the web. But the web will probably be intricate and irregular and messy. It will probably form a sort of hollow sphere about the earth. In particular, it will probably contain within itself a vast number of irregular rope 'circles' – that is to say, if you start from some particular flag and track along the ropes from pole to pole, always in a green–red direction, then you will often be able to get back to your starting-point again. Start from Flag One, in Naples, and proceed in a northerly direction, taking more or less a great circle route. Track along the ropes, some short and some long, moving from green to red, from green to red. Eventually, perhaps, you will recognize that you are in Bari, and a dozen more ropes will get you back to Flag One in Naples.

The point of the story is this. The numbered flags represent your beliefs. The planting of the flag-poles represents the acquisition of beliefs. Different geographical areas with different densities of flags represent different areas or topics, on some of which you will hold many beliefs and on others few. More importantly, the ropes are lines of justification. The direction of the ropes corresponds to the direction of justification. Thus if there is a rope with its green end tied to Flag One and its red end tied to Flag Seventeen, that models the thought that in your belief system proposition P_{17} is epistemically prior to proposition P_1 – that P_{17} is one of the set of belicfs which justifies your belief in P_1. If we follow out all the ropes tied by their green ends to Flag One and collect the flags at the red ends of these ropes, then we shall have collected the set Π_1 on which your belief that P_1 depends for its justification. The rope-web as a whole represents the tangle of justification which holds together the flags of your beliefs.

No flag-pole is tied to itself. That is to say, no belief is epistemically prior to itself. Again, if there is a green–red rope from one flag to another, then there is no other rope – and hence no red–green rope – from the second to the first. That is to say, the rules of roping presuppose that epistemic priority is asymmetrical. But epistemic priority will not be transitive. Let us see why this is so.

Take Flag One – F_1 – again, tied in green–red direction to F_{17}, which is (let us suppose) five miles away from it. Now F_{17} will, in turn, be tied in green–red direction to several further flags, including (say) F_{75}. Will F_1 also be tied to F_{75}? And if it is tied, will it be tied in green–red or in red–green direction? The answer is that the *rules* do not determine anything here. F_1 may or may not be tied, in either direction, to F_{75}. As a matter of fact, if F_{75} is more than a few hundred miles from F_1, which it perfectly well may be, then it will not be tied to F_1. But as far as the rules go, F_1 may or may not be tied, in either direction, to F_{75}. Any of three states is possible, states which can be pictured like this:

(1) G----------R (17) G----------R (75)
    G--------------------------R

(1) G----------R (17) G----------R (75)
    G--------------------------R

(1) G----------R (17) G----------R (75)

It should be clear what these pictures represent when flags are translated into beliefs and ropes into justificatory connexions.

The metaphor of the 'web of belief' has been used by some modern epistemologists.[14] They have pictured our belief systems,

---

14 Numerous models or analogies of this sort can be found in the literature. I take the phrase 'the web of belief' from W.V.O. Quine and J.S. Ullian, *The Web of Belief* (New York, 1970). But Quine's webs are like spiders' webs, and there can be a significant difference between their centres and their peripheries. My webs may have any configuration – they may be hollow spheres – and there need be nothing in them corresponding to the distinction between centre and periphery.

in more or less the fashion I have indicated, as a network of interconnected propositions, each proposition tied to several others, and the whole set forming an intricately interwoven mass. They have supposed that any particular belief is justified immediately by the other beliefs it is roped to, and that the belief system as a whole is justified in virtue of the whole intricate texture of the web – by the fact that each belief is roped to various other beliefs which are themselves roped to further beliefs, and so on.

This interweaving is, I take it, one way of understanding what have been called 'coherence' theories of knowledge or justification: what justifies my holding a particular belief is the fact that it is connected to other beliefs and thus forms part of a coherent belief system – the fact that it is connected, by various ropes, directly and indirectly, to all or most or many of my other beliefs. (The term 'coherence theory' has not been used to pick out any one determinate theory of knowledge – and often, or so I think, it has been used in a culpably vague fashion. I do not mean to say that my flag analogy pictures *the* coherence theory – only that it pictures one reasonably intelligible version of that 'theory' or cluster of theories.)

Coherence theorists have recognized that their views countenance, or seem likely to countenance, something rather like circular argumentation. Some theorists welcome this, saying that there is nothing wrong with a circular argument provided that the circle is 'large' enough (provided that any green–red journey from Naples back to Naples takes you past a reasonably large number of different flags). Other coherence theorists think that there must be objections to circular reasoning, and so they maintain that there are important differences between ordinary circles and the sort of circles which form parts of a web or net of beliefs. I cannot myself see that this is a significant disagreement. The interesting question is not whether the 'circularities' within a web are rightly *called* circles, but whether the circularities are vicious or virtuous. And that question turns, as I have said, on the nature of epistemic priority: in particular, on the transitivity or non-transitivity of the relation.

The picture of the web assumes (as I think virtually all epistemologists have assumed) that epistemic priority is asymmetrical. It also assumes that it is not transitive. Does it *show* that epistemic priority is asymmetrical but not transitive? Does it thereby show that at least some circular arguments may be acceptable? Of course it does not. A picture is not a proof. The rules of roping which I proposed have no special status. Other rules can quickly be invented, other pictures painted. But a picture or a model may have a persuasive, or even an illuminating, force. The model I have described purports to have such a force.

For our belief systems *are*, as a matter of fact, web-like in their structure. You will soon come to see this if you start reflecting on the beliefs you actually have. Kick the common philosophical habit of picking on beliefs one at a time and asking of each one why *it* is justified. Look instead at clumps of beliefs or, if you can, at the whole set of your beliefs: you will find (or so the model invites you to expect) that they do form a complex web, tied one to another in a messy and disorderly fashion by the cords of justification. And since this is what your belief system is actually like, and since it seems on the whole a reasonable and justifiable system, you will find that you must reject the supposed transitivity of epistemic priority. For your belief system is more or less reasonable; and it is incompatible with a transitive notion of epistemic priority.

Hence the story of the roped flag-poles gives us some reason for thinking – or suspecting – that epistemic priority is not transitive. At the very least, it gives us a reason for *hoping* that priority is not transitive. For if it is, then our actual beliefs which have no doubt been assembled in a splendidly rational manner will turn out to be an unreasonable muddle.

Consider a very simple example. It is a real example, not an artificially invented case. I believe that Galen wrote a commentary on Aristotle's *Categories*. My main reason for this belief is simply that Galen himself says that he wrote such a commentary. Why do I think that Galen says he wrote a commentary on the *Categories*? Because this statement is made in the *Institutio Logica*, which I believe to have been written by Galen. I believe that the *Institutio Logica* was written by Galen for several reasons: one of them, and the most obvious, is that the sole surviving manuscript of the work ascribes it to Galen. Now I believe *this* in part because I have a photograph of the manuscript on which I can read the letters ΛΛΗΝΟΥ, which I take to be the remains of ΓΑΛΗΝΟΥ ('Galen's'), and I take the photo to represent the manuscript reasonably accurately. I suppose that the photo is reasonably accurate because of certain beliefs about the way in which cameras work. And so on – the story could continue *ad libitum*, but enough of it has probably been told.

The question is this: Is my belief that Galen wrote a commentary on Aristotle's *Categories* justified, in part, by my belief that photographic film is light-sensitive? It seems to me that the answer is pretty clearly No. But if epistemic priority is transitive, then the answer to this and countless similar questions must be Yes. I do not insist on the conclusion that epistemic priority is not transitive. But I do insist that some strange and unwelcome consequences result from the thesis that it is transitive.

Where do we now stand? It is at best unclear whether epistemic priority is asymmetrical and transitive. Hence it is at best unclear whether or not the objection to circularity which we are considering is enough to show that epistemological circularities are intolerable. Of course, even if the objection fails, it does not follow that all circles – or even that any circles – are acceptable. Circularity is acceptable only if epistemic priority is not transitive. But if epistemic priority is not transitive, it does not follow that circularity is acceptable – there may be other objections to circles.

And so I shall end by briefly rehearsing a different objection, one which is frequently raised against coherence theories – and *a fortiori* against circular argumentation. The objection is closely parallel to an objection I considered in the previous chapter in connexion with infinite sequences of arguments or reasons. It runs like this.

Take any circle or web of beliefs, W. Let it be as complex as you like. Now construct a different web, W*, in the following fashion. Replace the constituent beliefs, all or some of them, by different and incompatible beliefs. (Replace 'Honey is sweet' and 'Naples is in Italy' by, say, 'Honey is bitter' and 'Naples is in Greece'.) Rope up the new beliefs in the same sort of way as you roped up the old – the ropings follow the same rules and exhibit the same complexity as before.

Now compare W with W*. In W we shall find a belief, P, which does not appear in W*. Instead, W* will contain some belief P*, which is incompatible with P. Now P was supposedly justified by its position in W – we were allegedly justified in believing that P by the fact that P was tied to or supported by numerous other propositions which were themselves tied and supported in turn. But W* has just the same structure, in all relevant respects, as W. Hence if P was justified by its position in W, P* will be justified by its position in W*. But we know that P and P* are incompatible with one another. Hence we cannot be justified in holding both of them. Hence we are justified in holding neither of them. And so, in sceptical fashion, we must suspend judgement.

In general, any appeal to W can be matched by an appeal to W*. One appeal succeeds if and only if the other appeal succeeds. But both appeals cannot succeed. Therefore neither appeal succeeds. Webs, or circles, are no better in this respect than infinite regressions.

Now a Dogmatist may object to this argument in exactly the same ways as he objected to the parallel argument about infinite sequences. The particular objection I want to set out is this. The sceptic in effect suggests that

> You may properly base your belief in P on its position in a web W only if you have reason to prefer W to any rival web W*.

The Dogmatist replies that, on the contrary,

> You may properly base your belief in P on its position in W, provided that W is in fact a true and coherent web; you do not need in addition to *know* that W is superior to W*.

The sceptical suggestion and the Dogmatic reply run parallel to the suggestions and replies which I rehearsed at the ends of the two previous chapters. Again, I postpone discussion.

But I may perhaps append a final observation, once again parallel to an observation at the end of the previous chapter. The objection to coherence theories which I have just sketched seems to have an almost irresistible pull. It is tempting to explain the pull by observing that webs and circles cannot justify beliefs because they appeal only to *other* beliefs – they do not link beliefs to *the world*. The web is, so to speak, detachable from the world; and for just that reason it cannot serve any warranting function.

As I said before, this line of thought must be resisted. Webs, like regressions, are (or so the Dogmatist may properly claim) linked to the world; for every flag is tied to a pole, and every pole is planted firmly in the earth. It is simply wrong to say that the beliefs which are roped to one another have no connexion with the world. The dialectical toing and froing at which I hinted at the end of the previous chapter may be practised in the same sort of way here too. But in the end I cannot see that the need to establish 'links with the world' will embarrass circular reasoners.

Although I find myself pulled by the objection from similar webs, and hence disinclined to give in to the seductive powers of the flagging game, I do not think I can yet produce a good *argument* which will either establish or refute the objection. Thus I end this lecture, as I ended the last, with a sort of temporizing scepticism: I cannot yet tell whether circular arguments should be shunned by philosophers.

4

Hypotheses

At the start of *M* III, his essay *Against the Geometers*, Sextus decides to deal with the so-called hypothetical method of geometrical proof. He observes that 'for the sake of orderly progress, we should realize at the beginning that things are called hypotheses in many different senses' (*M* III 3). Sextus is prudent; and since the subject of this chapter is the hypothetical mode of scepticism, I shall follow his example and first say something about the different sorts of things which the Greeks called hypotheses or about the different uses of the Greek word ὑπόθεσις.

Like Sextus, I shall leave aside the special senses which the word bears in rhetoric and in dramatic theory and focus on the senses which it has in logical and epistemological contexts. Even within logic, the word ὑπόθεσις was used in many ways. The different uses all have something in common – roughly speaking, an hypothesis is something which is set down or laid down or supposed. Thus Philoponus can use the word ὑπόθεσις to denote the antecedent of a conditional proposition (e.g. *in APr* 243.15–24) – in a conditional, you 'lay down' the antecedent and see what follows. Similarly, Proclus can use the word ὑπόθεσις to denote the subject-term of a universal affirmative proposition (e.g. *in Eucl* 252.5–23) – in saying 'All isosceles triangles have their base-angles equal', you 'suppose' you have an isosceles triangle and 'conclude' to the equality of its base-angles.

Neither of these sorts of 'laying down' or 'supposing' concerns me here. I am interested in cases where an hypothesis is a complete utterance, not part of an utterance. A good starting-point is the Stoic classification of utterances. For the Stoics distinguished what they called an 'hypothetical' kind of utterance. Although our sources do not say much about this kind of utterance, they do give some helpful illustrations. Thus according to Ammonius,

> the Stoics say that there is an hypothetical kind of utterance, e.g. 'Let it be laid down (ὑποκείσθω) that the earth is the centre of the solar sphere'. *(in Int* 2.31–2)

And the Stoic Epictetus provides the following example:

> We should behave in life as we do in the case of hypothetical utterances. 'Let it be night'. Let it be (ἔστω). 'Well, then, is it day?' No; for I assumed the hypothesis of its being night. 'Let it be that you think that it is night'. Let it be. 'Then take it that it *is* night'. That does not follow from the hypothesis.
> *(diss* I xxv 11–13)

Thus it appears that the characteristic mark of an hypothetical utterance is an initial third person imperative: 'Let it be supposed', 'Let it be', ὑποκείσθω, ἔστω. This is confirmed by Sextus, who speaks of 'the mathematicians who assume by hypothesis the first principles of their proofs and theorems, saying "Let it be granted (δεδόσθω)"' *(M* III 17). Sextus plainly takes 'Let it be that...' as the mark of an hypothetical utterance; and he plainly takes hypothetical utterances to be the canonical way of expressing hypotheses.

Then an hypothetical utterance has the form: 'Let it be the case that P'. The hypothesis itself is the content of the utterance: in saying 'Let it be the case that P', you hypothesize – you lay it down as an hypothesis – that P; and what you hypothesize, viz. that P, is the hypothesis. Hypotheses are not in any normal sense a *class* of propositions; for we cannot intelligibly ask, in the abstract, whether or not a given proposition is an hypothesis. A proposition is an hypothesis when, and in the context in which, it is hypothesized; and it is thus an hypothesis not absolutely and without qualification, but relatively and within a determinate context of discourse. Is the proposition that it is night an hypothesis? The question is misconceived. Has the proposition that it is night ever been advanced as an hypothesis? Yes – in the little discussion which Epictetus reports or invents.

It may seem to follow that anything at all may be hypothesized; for surely I may sensibly say 'Let it be that P' for any proposition P whatsoever? (By 'sensibly' I mean 'without syntactic or semantic impropriety': what we may hypothesize sensibly in the sense of 'advisedly' is another matter.) In a way this is true, and it is a truth which Sextus will exploit to the full in the hypothetical mode. (It is also a truth important to and familiar from many modern systems of formal logic. For 'natural deduction' systems standardly contain a 'rule of assumption', and such a rule, in the words of one textbook, 'permits us to introduce at *any* stage of an argument *any* proposition we choose as an assumption of the argument'. Sextus will not be showing himself captiously or idiosyncratically Pyrrhonian if he insists that we may hypothesize anything whatsoever.) But if you may hypothesize absolutely anything so far as the *form* of the hypothesis goes, the purpose and function of hypothesizing may yet put constraints on the content of permissible hypotheses.

What is – what was – the function of hypotheses? Here the Greeks had two distinct traditions. The first tradition may be called Platonic, since it is best known from certain famous passages in Plato's dialogues.[1] In the Platonic tradition, hypothesizing has primarily an heuristic function. You are interested in some problem or question, say the question: Can virtue be taught? In order to make progress towards an answer to the question, you venture some hypothesis. Perhaps you hypothesize or suppose ('for the sake of argument') that virtue is a kind of knowledge. You next see whether, granted the hypothesis, you can answer the original question. If you can, you proceed to worry about the hypothesis itself, asking whether virtue is in fact a kind of knowledge. And you will typically tackle this question by advancing a second hypothesis.

The details of the Platonic tradition of hypothesizing are controversial. But its general features are, for present purposes, clear enough. Plato's hypothetical method is, as I said, an heuristic device; and that fact determines the nature of the hypothesizing which it involves. Thus, first, although you may in principle hypothesize anything, in practice the context of the business and the form of the question in hand will determine that some hypotheses are better and more useful than others. (If the question is,

---

1 I mean the reflections on the 'hypothetical method' at *Meno* 86D–87B; *Phaedo* 100A–101E; *Republic* 510B–511E. (Plato did not himself invent the method: he adapted it from contemporary geometrical practice.)

Can virtue be taught?, it will evidently be fruitless to hypothesize that the price of wheat will rise next year.) Secondly, in hypothesizing that P, you do not commit yourself to the *truth* of P, nor do you *assert* that P. You may, of course, hope – or even expect – that it will turn out that your hypothesis is true. But in the nature of things, many hypotheses will turn out to be false, and you will abandon them: in doing so, you are not going back on anything you said or changing your mind. (In the special case of *reductio ad absurdum* proofs, you may positively hope that the hypothesis will turn out to be false; for you hypothesize that P, and then try to derive a contradiction or an absurdity, which will allow you to *deny* that P. Here you are evidently not asserting that P or committing yourself to the truth of P when you say 'Let it be the case that P'.) Thirdly, in hypothesizing that P, you do not *argue* for P or produce any sort of reason in favour of it. Later, of course, you may look for reasons in support of the proposition you had previously hypothesized; but insofar as you produce reasons and argue that P, to that extent you do not offer P as an hypothesis. Indeed, one of the points of saying 'Let it be the case that P' (rather than simply 'P') is precisely to indicate that P is being put forward – at least *pro tempore* – without argument or grounds.

The second tradition of hypothesizing I shall call Aristotelian. Aristotle himself used the word ὑπόθεσις in a variety of ways, but one use had a particular importance. For Aristotle held that among the first principles or ἀρχαί on which any science is based there will be hypotheses (*APst* 72a20–4). Hypotheses are, in this sense, a species of what we tend to call axioms, the first or primary or primitive principles from which the remaining truths or theorems of a science are derived. This Aristotelian usage had an afterlife. Proclus, for example, uses the word ὑπόθεσις in what he takes to be the Aristotelian way in order to characterize a subdivision of the axioms of Euclid's geometry (*in Eucl* 76.24). But the precise delineation of this special Aristotelian sense need not detain us; for the term ὑπόθεσις came to be used more generously, so that *all* first principles, and not merely a subgroup of them, could be called hypotheses. I shall call this use the broad Aristotelian use of the term (though it is not clear that the use is to be found in Aristotle himself).

Proclus records the broad Aristotelian usage:

Axioms, postulates and hypotheses are distinguished according to Aristotle's own exposition. Often, however, all these things [i.e. all first principles] are called hypotheses.

(*in Eucl* 76.24–77.3; cf. 178.1–14)

A similar remark is found some centuries earlier from the pen of the Peripatetic scholarch, Alexander of Aphrodisias:

Hypotheses are first principles of proofs, because there is no proof of such propositions, i.e. of first principles, but they are posited as evident and known in themselves (αὐτόθεν)..., and what is assumed without proof they call an hypothesis (or even, more generally, a thesis) and say that it is hypothesized.

(*in APr* 13.7–11)

This broad Aristotelian use of ὑπόθεσις is not common in early writers; but Proclus and Alexander were recording a usage, not inventing one, and the word is found not infrequently in later Greek texts in just this sense.[2]

The Aristotelian form of hypothesizing has one important feature in common with the Platonic form: in hypothesizing that P you do not *argue* that P or produce any reason in favour of holding that P. (As I said, this feature is characteristic of hypothetical utterances as such and is implicit in their canonical mode of expression.) But the explanation of this feature of hypothesizing is quite different in the Aristotelian case. In the Platonic case, you hypothesize that P as part of an heuristic strategy and you may well proceed later to argue that P. In the Aristotelian case, hypothesizing is not an heuristic but a demonstrative activity: in hypothesizing that P you lay it down, as a first principle, that P; and your hypothesis is not a mid-point in the search for truth but a starting-point in the demonstration of truth. You do not argue that P, because, if P is indeed a first principle, you *cannot* argue that P. Aristotelian hypotheses are things for which no argument is possible. They are not temporarily unsupported (as they are for Plato) but necessarily unsupportable. They are 'evident and known in themselves', as Alexander puts it. They cannot, trivially and by definition, be known on the basis of anything else; and it is for this reason that you will not argue – ever

---

2 A few examples from Sextus: *PH* I 183; *M* IX 2, 419; *M* VI 5 (τὰς ἀρχικὰς ὑποθέσεις); from Galen: *sect ingred* I 93 K; *us part* III 45–6 K; *loc aff* VIII 324, 316 K; *lib prop* XIX 43 K.

– for your Aristotelian hypotheses. I stress this point. It will become important.

It is clear, too, that in making an Aristotelian hypothesis you are committing yourself to a truth. In laying down something as a first principle, you are thereby supposing that it is *true*; and if it emerges that the hypothesis is false – that the proposition you took to be an hypothesis is not even *true*, let alone a first truth – then you were mistaken and your hypothesizing was an error. Aristotelian hypothesizing is a sort of asserting.

Finally, you will not – of course – be prepared to hypothesize *anything*. In hypothesizing that P, you are taking P to be a first principle. Not every proposition, not even every true proposition, can function as the first principle of a science.

Platonic hypotheses and Aristotelian hypotheses are thus two very different birds. And it is Aristotelian hypotheses, broad Aristotelian hypotheses, with which the Pyrrhonists were concerned. In *M* III, Sextus remarks that

> in a third sense, we call hypotheses the first principles (ἀρχαί) of proofs; for an hypothesis is the postulating (αἴτησις) of a fact for the establishing of something. (*M* III 4)

This, he says, is the sort of hypothesis which he is going to investigate (*M* III 6).

M III is directed specifically against the geometers. We might find it surprising that the geometers should be taken to use *Aristotelian* hypotheses. For Plato associated *his* hypothetical method with geometrical practice, and we ourselves might be inclined to think that Platonic rather than Aristotelian hypotheses were the stuff of geometry. But when Sextus talks of the hypothetical method of the geometers, he has in mind a method of proof which begins by laying down, or hypothesizing, certain propositions as first principles:

> the geometers, seeing the mass of problems which dog them, retreat into what they think to be a matter safe and free from danger, namely the postulating of their geometrical first principles by hypothesis. (*M* III 1)

As far as Sextus is concerned – and hence as far as we are concerned – the geometers' hypotheses are ἀρχαί, Aristotelian hypotheses.

Nor is Sextus being perverse or unfair; for the definition of hypotheses which he gives at *M* III 4 was lifted *verbatim* from a geometrical textbook. (We happen to know this because a learned bishop of Laodicea by chance copied the very same text into his notebook.³)

Although in *M* III Sextus is gunning for geometry, he does not suppose that the hypothetical method is peculiar to the geometers. Indeed, he characterizes hypotheses at *M* III 4 in entirely general terms, and he illustrates the type of hypothesis he has in mind by rehearsing the three principles on which the doctor Asclepiades hoped to ground medical science (*M* III 5). Elsewhere Sextus observes that

> it is not only proofs but pretty well the whole of philosophy which the Dogmatists claim to advance by way of hypothesis.
>
> (*M* VIII 369)

And he is right. The Dogmatists did indeed suppose that all φιλοσοφία, all knowledge, depends ultimately on ἀρχαί or ὑποθέσεις. And in attacking the hypothetical method and the claims of hypothesizers, Sextus is attacking the foundations of all Dogmatic knowledge.

The attack employs what Sextus calls the hypothetical mode of scepticism or the mode 'from an hypothesis' (*PH* I 164, 168). This mode is adduced more often than any other form of Agrippan argumentation, διαφωνία excepted: it is discussed and justified thrice, and it is employed on some forty or fifty occasions in Sextus' different writings. The prevalence of the hypothetical mode might be doubted; for in fact Sextus refers to ὑποθέσεις by name on very few occasions indeed.⁴ But the doubt would be mistaken – there are numerous *implicit* references to hypotheses in his writings. It is worth dwelling on the matter for a moment.

Sextus begins his discussion of hypotheses in *M* III by remarking that

---

3 The bishop was Anatolius; the text in question is most easily found in volume IV of J.L. Heiberg's Teubner edition of Hero (Leipzig, 1912): *Definitions* 138.8 (= p.166.4–16). See Karel Janáček, "Ὁ ἐξ ὑποθέσεως τρόπος', *Eirene* 25, 1987, 55–65.

4 Outside the discussions of the hypothetical method and mode (*PH* I 168, 173–4; *M* VIII 369–78; *M* III 1–17) see *PH* I 177, 186; II 20; *M* VIII 343, 367. (In addition, Sextus sometimes uses the word ὑπόθεσις in other contexts where the hypothetical mode is not at issue.)

Hypotheses

those who assume something by hypothesis and without proof are satisfied by a bare assertion (ψιλή φάσις) alone.

(M III 7)

A 'bare' assertion is not a type of assertion; to make a bare assertion is to make an assertion barely – it is *merely* to assert.[5] Sextus supposes that hypothesizers *assert*, and do *nothing more* than assert. This supposition is – or seems at first blush to be – justified. For, as I explained, Aristotelian hypothesizers do indeed commit themselves to the truth of what they hypothesize (they produce a φάσις); but they do not offer any argument or reason for the hypothesis (they produce a ψιλή φάσις).

Now the fact that hypotheses are bare assertions is, for the sceptics, the central fact about them. Hence Sextus will often use the phrase ψιλή φάσις when he wishes to refer to an ὑπόθεσις – and usually where the phrase ψιλή φάσις occurs the hypothetical mode of ἐποχή is being invoked.[6] Moreover, since a ψιλή φάσις is simply a φάσις – since a bare assertion is simply an assertion – Sextus can use the term φάσις, without qualification, to advert to an hypothesis: the context will make it clear that when he says 'They use a φάσις', he means 'They use a bare φάσις', i.e. 'They use an ὑπόθεσις'.[7]

Making a bare assertion contrasts with offering an argument or reason for your assertion. In Sextus, the contrast is often explicitly drawn; for Sextus often uses the hypothetical mode in conjunction with some other sceptical mode in order to produce a dilemma for the Dogmatist: 'Either he makes the bare assertion that P, or else he argues that P.' (The contrast is usually between making a bare assertion and offering a proof or ἀπόδειξις;[8] but other contrasts also occur.[9]) This provides Sextus with another way of referring to

5 For comparable uses of ψιλός in Sextus see e.g. M VII 376 (a ψιλή ἀλλοίωσις, a change and nothing more); VIII 476 (a ψιλή θέσις, merely entertaining a thought without assenting to it); M I 49 (a ψιλή γνῶσις, merely knowing your letters without being able to explain their discovery or their nature).
6 For ψιλή φάσις see *PH* II 121; M VII 315; VIII 15, 76, 368, 435/6; M III 7. Note the synonymous phrase, ψιλή ὑπόσχεσις, at M III 179, 259.
7 For φάσις see *PH* II 107, 153; M VII 315, 337, 339; VIII 61, 281, 360, 444; M I 157, 188, 279. Note also ἀποφαίνεται μόνον at M VIII 15.
8 ᾿Απόδειξις is the contrast at *PH* I 60, 114/5, 122, 173; II 107, 121, 153; M VII 315, 339; VIII 15, 61, 76, 78, 281, 343, 374, 463/4; M I 157, 188, 279; II 109; III 7, 8, 12, 13, 34.
9 Contrast with κριτήριον: *PH* 88; M VII 337, 440; VIII 26; with λόγος: M VIII 120, 463; with ὑπόμνησις: M VIII 444; with ἔφοδος or μέθοδος: M VIII 436.

97

hypotheses. For instead of writing 'Either a bare assertion or a proof', he will often write 'Either no proof or a proof' to make exactly the same point. So that in some contexts the phrase 'no proof' or the like must count as an implicit reference to hypothesizing and an implicit invocation of the hypothetical mode.[10] Thus Sextus has a variety of ways of adverting to the notion of an hypothesis. And the fact – a mildly curious fact – that he rarely adverts to the notion by using the term ὑπόθεσις is perfectly consistent with the fact that he frequently refers to Dogmatic hypothesizing.

Sextus' references to Dogmatic hypothesizing are all of them hostile; and it is the hypothetical mode which he employs in his attacks upon this hypothesizing. The mode is named at *PH* I 164 and formally described at I 168:

> The mode from an hypothesis occurs when the Dogmatists, being thrown back *ad infinitum*, begin from something which they do not establish but claim to assume simply and without proof by virtue of an agreement.

The description is less than illuminating. He says *when* the hypothetical mode will be adduced, viz. whenever the Dogmatists attempt to escape from an infinite regression. But he does not say *what* the mode is – he does not here explain *why* the sceptic objects to Aristotelian hypothesizing or *how* the mode is supposed to reduce hypothesizers to ἐποχή.

Moreover, even the account of *when* the hypothetical mode is used seems to be false: Sextus implies that the Dogmatists only hypothesize when they are being threatened with an infinite regression, so that the dilemma they confront should always take the form 'Either you barely assert or else an infinite regression follows'. But the Dogmatists are not invariably confronted by that particular dilemma – it is one of several dilemmas which Sextus sets for them.

---

10 See *PH* I 60, 122; II 34, 54, 85, 113, 121; III 34; *M* VIII 436 (all using ἀναπόδεικτος, ἄνευ ἀποδείξεως, or the like). Also *PH* I 114; *M* VII 440; VIII 120 (ἀκρίτως cf. *PH* II 88, ἀνεπικρίτως (if the text is sound)); and *PH* III 23; *M* IX 204 (χωρὶς αἰτίας). Note also the common use of αὐτόθεν in this context to point a contrast with μετ' ἀποδείξεως: *M* VIII 26, 28, 75, 120, 343, 371; *M* II 109; III 9; and cf. ἐξ ἑτοίμου at *M* VIII 26, 78.

The remark about when to use the hypothetical mode is absent from the account in Diogenes Laertius (IX 89), and perhaps it was an ill-judged addition by Sextus himself.[11] (Otherwise the description in Diogenes is in substance the same: there are some minor differences in expression, which would repay examination; but I do not think that they have any effect on the philosophical understanding of the mode.)

Sextus nowhere explains why the hypothetical mode should be thought to further the ends of the sceptic, why it is a mode of ἐποχή. But part of the answer should be apparent from my discussion of the two previous modes. If the only thing that can be said for or against P is that some Dogmatist has hypothesized it, and if hypothesizing that P does not establish or warrant belief in P, then we should suspend judgement over P. The doctor Asclepiades hypothesized his three ἀρχαί, and thought thereby to establish his medical science. He did nothing more. But hypothesizing, as the hypothetical mode allegedly shows, is a valueless procedure. Hence, as far as Asclepiades' hypothesizing goes, ὅσον ἐπὶ τούτῳ, we should suspend judgement about his ἀρχαί. There is thus a parallel between the hypothetical mode and the modes of regression and reciprocity: each of them leads to scepticism by way of a qualifying ὅσον ἐπὶ τούτῳ. But I shall show later how the hypothetical mode is also tied in a more intimate way to suspension of judgement.

Sextus does give us, at least implicitly, an explanation of what the hypothetical mode consists in. For at *PH* I 173–4, in the middle of his illustrative example of how the Five Modes of Agrippa may work together to achieve suspension of judgement, Sextus somewhat inappropriately offers three arguments against the reasonableness of using Aristotelian hypotheses. The three arguments reappear at *M* VIII 369–78, where they are joined by a fourth argument, which is interpolated between the second and the third arguments of the *PH* text, and also by a rebuttal of a Dogmatic counter-argument. And at *M* III 7–17 the four arguments of *M* VIII, together with the rebuttal, reappear. The arguments which support the hypothetical mode implicitly explain what it is.

---

11 So Karel Janáček, 'Skeptische Zweitropenlehre und Sextus Empiricus', *Eirene* 8, 1970, 47–55.

The three texts to which I have referred are very close to one another, in language as well as in content. There can be no doubt that they are all drawn from the same source, which Sextus copied three times with greater or less fidelity. I myself suspect that the version in *M* III is closest in content to the source, and hence that Sextus took his attack on hypotheses from an earlier sceptical discussion of geometrical method.[12] It is at least possible that this source was an essay by Agrippa himself. But this is speculation, and speculation of a pretty pointless kind.

Better turn to the arguments. I shall first outline the four arguments of *M* VIII and *M* III, and then comment upon them. The rebuttal I leave until later.

(1) If it is acceptable for a Dogmatist to hypothesize that P, i.e. to lay down P, by a bare assertion, as a first principle or ἀρχή, then it must be equally acceptable for a sceptic – or another Dogmatist – to hypothesize that P*, where P* is the 'opposite' of P. But if P* is no less acceptable than P, we cannot accept P as a first principle just because the Dogmatist hypothesizes it. (See *PH* I 173; *M* VIII 370; *M* III 8.)

(2) What the Dogmatists hypothesize is either true or false. If it is true, they should not *hypothesize* it (for hypothesis is 'a matter full of suspicion') but rather assume it straight off. If it is false, it can do them no good – for a false starting-point cannot ground a science or a branch of knowledge. (See *PH* I 173; *M* VIII 371; *M* III 9–10.)

(3) If the Dogmatists hold that the consequences of any hypothesis are acceptable, then all enquiry is subverted. For, given any absurd proposition, we can find some hypothesis from which it follows; hence any proposition whatsoever will be acceptable. And this is evidently silly. (See *M* VIII 372–3; *M* III 11–12.)

(4) If in order to establish that P_2 you first hypothesize that P_1 and then derive P_2 from P_1, why not establish P_2 directly, by hypothesizing *it*, and thus save yourself the labour of looking for arguments? (See *PH* I 174; *M* VIII 374; *M* III 13.)

The second of these four arguments is curious, for two reasons. No doubt any hypothesis is either true or false; and no doubt any false hypothesis is a 'rotten foundation' (*M* III 10). But what is wrong with a true hypothesis? Sextus alleges that hypothesis is 'a thing full of suspicion' (*M* VIII 371; *M* III 9). But the argument he is

---

12 For a contrary view, see Janáček, "Ὁ ἐξ ὑποθέσεως τρόπος".

offering us is designed precisely to show that hypothesizing is a suspect business – and it is odd to argue that hypotheses are suspect by assuming that they are suspect. You might perhaps imagine that Sextus is reporting some widespread suspicion of the hypothetical method: 'People as a rule look askance at hypotheses – so don't make them if you can avoid them.' But it seems to me unlikely that Sextus means to offer this sociological observation; and even if he does, it will carry little weight. No decent Dogmatist will worry much if laymen regard his procedures with suspicion. What matters is that they are scientifically legitimate, not that they get a favourable press.

The second curiosity about the argument is yet more puzzling. If what you hypothesize is true, Sextus urges, then 'you should assume it directly as true (αὐτόθεν λαμβάνειν ὡς ἀληθές)' (*M* VIII 371; *M* III 9); for 'no one hypothesizes what is true and is the case' (*M* III 9). But whatever can be the contrast between hypothesizing something on the one hand and 'directly' assuming it as true on the other? Sextus himself characterizes hypothesizing in terms of assuming in his initial description at *PH* I 168; and he frequently uses the adverb 'directly (αὐτόθεν)' in allusions to hypotheses.[13] If a Dogmatist hypothesizes that P, then he thereby assumes directly, i.e. without argument, that P is true; and if a Dogmatist assumes directly that P is true, then he thereby hypothesizes that P. Hypothesizing and directly assuming are one and the same thing. Sextus' contrast is false – and perplexing. (It is true that some Dogmatists made terminological distinctions between hypotheses and assumptions; but these technical distinctions are – so far as I can see – of no relevance at all to Sextus' argument.)

I cannot find any way to make the second of Sextus' arguments even mildly plausible. Nor can I discover any persuasive explanation of how Sextus might have come to advance this bewildering line of thought.

The remaining three arguments rely each on a similar supposition. The first argument supposes that if you may hypothesize that P, then you may equally hypothesize that P* (where P* is an 'opposite' of P). The fourth argument supposes that if you may hypothesize that P, then you may equally hypothesize anything

---

13 See the references in n.10.

which follows from P. And the third argument supposes – or seems to suppose – that if you may hypothesize that P, then you may equally hypothesize anything at all: that if you may hypothesize one thing, then you may hypothesize any thing. If that is so, then we might consider the third argument to be, in effect, a general argument of which the first and the fourth are specific instances.

It might be doubted that the third argument does make the wholly general supposition that if you may hypothesize one thing you may hypothesize any thing. What Sextus actually affirms is that 'if someone claims that whatever follows from what is assumed by hypothesis is firm, then he confounds all philosophical enquiry' (*M* VIII 372). He offers two particular illustrations: let us hypothesize that three is equal to four (*M* VIII 372; *M* III 11), or let us hypothesize that what is in motion is at rest (*M* III 12). And he points out that in each case we shall get lunatic results. Both examples are cases of inconsistent or self-contradictory hypotheses; so perhaps the third argument supposes that if you may hypothesize that P, then you may hypothesize (not anything at all, but) some *inconsistent* proposition. Yet it is hard to see how this supposition could be made plausible. How could anyone think that if he accepted any one piece of hypothesizing then he would have to accept some inconsistent hypothesis but would not have to accept every hypothesis whatever? Surely, if something is going to oblige you to allow an inconsistent hypothesis, it will oblige you to allow any hypothesis at all? So I incline to think after all that the third argument does tacitly make the utterly general supposition that if one hypothesis is acceptable then any hypothesis is acceptable.

However that may be, it is plain how the Dogmatist will attempt to rebut Sextus' third argument. For he will certainly deny the general supposition that if you may hypothesize one proposition you may hypothesize any proposition. And he will certainly deny the specific supposition that if any hypothesis is acceptable then some inconsistent hypothesis must be acceptable. Indeed, he will surely maintain that no inconsistent hypothesis is acceptable – and for an obvious reason. Any inconsistent proposition is thereby false; and Aristotelian hypotheses are advanced as truths. Therefore no inconsistent proposition may be acceptably hypothesized.

And a Dogmatist will react in a similar way to the fourth of Sextus' arguments. The Dogmatist wishes to establish that P$_2$

(where it is under investigation or in dispute whether or not P_2). He adduces the hypothesis that P_1 from which he will proceed to show that P_2. Sextus retorts that if you are ready to hypothesize that P_1 you may with equal justice hypothesize that P_2.

> If what is hypothesized is firm and reliable *qua* hypothesized, then let the Dogmatic philosophers hypothesize not the points from which they infer the unclear item but rather the unclear item itself, i.e. not the premisses of the proof but the conclusion. But let them hypothesize this ten thousand times over, it will not be warranted, because it is unclear and because it is under investigation. So it is evident too that if they postulate the premisses of the proof without proof, they achieve nothing towards warranting them, because they too are matters of controversy. (*M* VIII 374)

The argument here is compressed. Sextus takes a Dogmatist to argue for P_2 by offering the following proof: 'P_1; so P_2'. And the Dogmatist is supposed to advance P_1 as an hypothesis. The Sextan retort is this: 'Then why not hypothesize P_2 directly?' 'Plainly', comes the reply, 'this will not do; for P_2 is unclear and under investigation – it needs argument, not bare assertion.' 'Well then,' concludes the sceptic, 'you may not hypothesize P_1 either – for P_1 will also be under investigation and a matter of controversy.'

There are two oddities about this argument. First, Sextus does not explain why he thinks that P_1 will be under dispute. He supposes that any and every hypothesized proposition will be a matter of controversy, but he does not say why he makes this strong supposition. I can only imagine that he is tacitly invoking the mode of disagreement, or rather the claim made in the presentation of that mode that everything is subject to disagreement or διαφωνία. If everything is under dispute, then everything hypothesized will be under dispute. Now since whatever is subject to disagreement is ἄδηλον or unclear, and since a Dogmatist will not hypothesize what is unclear, nothing can be hypothesized. (If this is what Sextus has in mind, then the hypothetical mode is here made to depend for its efficacy on the mode of disagreement.)

Secondly, it is not clear that the Dogmatist can only justify his refusal to hypothesize P_2 by appealing to the fact that P_2 is unclear and a matter of investigation. Surely he might instead – and better – offer a formal reason for refusing to hypothesize P_2. He might hold that if a proposition is provable, then it may not be hypothesized. For Aristotelian hypotheses are intended to be offered as first principles; hence they cannot be proved. So if there is a good argument from P_1 (or from any other proposition) to P_2, you should not hypothesize that P_2; for P_2 cannot then be a first principle. (Matters are in fact a little more complicated than this; but it is clear that a purely formal criterion will rule out at any rate *some* of the hypothesizings which the Pyrrhonist wishes upon the Dogmatist.)

In both the fourth and the third arguments, then, Sextus makes a supposition of the form 'If it is legitimate to hypothesize P, then it is legitimate to hypothesize X'. The Dogmatist will reject both suppositions; and – which is the important point here – he may do so on purely formal or logical grounds. For he may say, against the fourth argument, that if P_2 can be proved from P_1, then P_2 may not be hypothesized. And he may say, against the third argument, that if a proposition is self-contradictory (if it entails something of the form 'P and not-P'), then it may not be hypothesized.

Up to this point, ὅσον ἐπὶ τούτῳ, the Dogmatist surely has a case. I do not wish to suggest that Sextus has no possible answer to the case. But I think that any answer will in effect lead into the first of Sextus' four arguments against hypothesizing, the argument to which I now turn.

It is plain from our texts that the first argument is the chief and most important of the four. Outside the three passages in which Sextus discusses the faults of hypothesizing, he never alludes to the second or to the third of his arguments, and he alludes only once to the fourth (*M* VIII 343). But he frequently refers to the first argument, thereby suggesting that he thinks it the best or most persuasive argument – perhaps, indeed, that it is in itself constitutive of the hypothetical mode.[14]

Moreover, he twice says that this argument was actually used, and therefore accepted, by the Dogmatists themselves (*M* VIII 360, 463). In both passages Sextus refers generically to οἱ δογματικοί: he neither names actual Dogmatists nor cites actual texts. Some scholars may be led to wonder if the passages really warrant our

---

14 See *PH* II 107, 153; III 23; *M* VII 315, 337; VIII 15, 26, 28, 76, 78, 120, 281, 360, 436, 463; *M* I 157, 188.

making the historical claim that 'the Dogmatists' in fact adduced and accepted Sextus' first argument; and they may observe that Sextus, like any other philosophical controversialist, will often say in a dialectical context 'They state that so-and-so', without intending his remarks in any rigorously historical sense. This is true. None the less, the two texts do give us *some* reason for thinking that Sextus' first argument was also used by some Dogmatists. And it is, of course, a thoroughly Pyrrhonian practice to turn Dogmatic weapons against the Dogmatists.

Sextus' account of the first argument runs like this:

> If what they say they assume by hypothesis is warranted because it is assumed by hypothesis, then its opposite (ἐναντίον), when assumed by hypothesis, will also appear warranted – and in this way we shall hypothesize conflicting things. And if in the latter case – I mean, in the case of the opposites – the hypothesis is weak in warranty, then it will be weak too in the former case, so that this time we shall hypothesize neither. (*M* VIII 370; cf. *M* III 8)

Here Sextus uses the word ἐναντίον, 'opposite'. Elsewhere, and more often, he employs ἀντικείμενον ('contradictory') or one of its cognates. The two words are to be taken as synonyms, and they are to be construed in a generous sense: P* is 'opposite' or 'contradictory' to P just in case it conflicts (μάχεται) with P (cf. *PH* I 10, 190). The essential thought is this: P and P* are opposites provided that the truth of the one excludes the truth of the other.[15] (Usually, Sextus writes as though any claim must have exactly one 'opposite'. But he should not be held to this thought, and his argument will be unaffected if we allow that a claim may have several 'opposites'.)

Thus the argument is this. Suppose a Dogmatist hypothesizes that P. Then there will always be some proposition P*, an 'opposite' of P or incompatible with it, which we may hypothesize (or which someone else may hypothesize or indeed actually has hypothesized). Suppose, then, that hypothesizing that P warrants the Dogmatist in affirming that P and warrants our believing his affirmation. Then hypothesizing that P* must warrant the affirmation and legitimate the belief that P*. Hence we shall hypothesize –

15 For the notion of conflict see note 12 to Chapter 1.

and be warranted in believing – both P and P*. But P and P* conflict with one another; and since we know them to conflict, we cannot be justified in believing both of them to be true. Suppose, then, that we therefore reject P*, holding that hypothesizing it gave us after all no grounds for belief. Then we must equally reject P, for exactly the same reason.

The argument is clear, and its conclusion irresistible, *provided* that the general principle implicit in it is true. The general principle is this: for any proposition P there is a proposition P* such that (i) P and P* are mutually incompatible, and (ii) hypothesizing that P will give warranty to P just in case hypothesizing that P* will give warranty to P*.

Now it is evident that any Dogmatist will deny, and hope to refute, this general principle. He will of course allow that for any P there is an incompatible P*; but he will maintain that if it is legitimate to hypothesize P, then it is *not* legitimate to hypothesize P*. He will claim, in short, that he is entitled and able to *choose* among putative hypotheses.

Sextus is perfectly aware of this. In connexion with his third argument, after he has himself pretended to hypothesize that three is equal to four and that what moves is at rest, he notes:

> And just as the geometers will say that these hypotheses are out of place (for the foundation must be firm if what follows is to be agreed upon), so we ourselves will refuse to admit without proof anything which they assume hypothetically.
>
> (*M* III 12; cf. VIII 373)

The Dogmatists – here, the geometers – are made to say explicitly that not any putative hypotheses may legitimately be hypothesized: some hypotheses are 'out of place', and the wise man will choose among potential hypotheses. The same point is made in a passage of Epictetus. Epictetus is discussing the question: What is the point of studying logic? He answers that errors in reasoning are immoral and 'against one's duty (παρὰ τὸ καθῆκον)', and that they can only be avoided by studying logic.

> And the same is true of hypotheses and hypothetical utterances. Sometimes it is necessary to postulate (αἰτῆσαι) an hypothesis as a sort of basis for the ensuing argument. Now

should one accept every offered hypothesis? And if not every
one, then which?   (*diss* I vii 22–3)

Epictetus clearly means that we should *not* accept 'every offered
hypothesis'; and he implies that studying logic will enable us to
answer the crucial question, 'And if not every hypothesis, then
which?'. Thus Epictetus is in effect saying that one of the main
benefits of Stoic logic is that it can provide an answer to the
hypothetical mode of the Pyrrhonists. (And I like to think – though
it may be deemed rash to do so – that Epictetus was actually aware
of the problem posed for Stoic philosophy by the hypothetical
mode of the Pyrrhonists.)

Now why should Sextus suppose that it would be difficult to find
an answer to the crucial question? Why should he think that the
selection of hypotheses is a difficult – even an impossible – matter?

We might expect him to have noted that his first argument
against the hypothetical method is more threatening than the third
or fourth arguments in the following way. All three arguments rely,
as I have noted, on some general principle to the effect that if you
may properly hypothesize P then you may equally hypothesize X.
In the case of the third and the fourth arguments, the Dogmatists
could (or so it seemed) offer a purely formal criterion on the basis of
which the relevant principles could be rejected and the Sextan
argument evaded. But in the case of the first argument no formal
criterion offers itself. True, we may properly take it as a formal
principle that if P and P* conflict, then both may not be hypothesized. But no formal criterion will enable us to determine which
of several conflicting hypotheses (if any) we may legitimately advance. Now you may say that there is nothing especially desirable
about finding a *formal* criterion for rejecting putative hypotheses:
any criterion will do, formal or informal. I agree. But it is in fact far
easier to hit upon formal criteria, and far easier to commend them,
than it is to formulate and make persuasive an informal criterion.

However that may be, Sextus himself does not advance this
consideration. He has, I think, a simpler and more general point in
mind. It emerges from the following text – one of the many
passages in which the hypothetical mode is applied.

> The Dogmatist will not simply assert. For then one of his
> opponents will utter the assertion which claims the opposite,

and in this way the former will be no more warranted than the
latter – for one bare assertion is worth the same as another.

(*M* VII 315)

The crucial sentence is the last sentence: 'one bare assertion is
worth the same as another'. Since P and P* are each bare assertions,
they have the same worth; they are, as Sextus says elsewhere,
equipollent or ἰσοσθενής (*M* VIII 436). But in that case, as Sextus
asks at *M* VIII 120, 'why should we assent to one rather than to the
other?' We have no reason to prefer P to P* or *vice versa*; and as for
the Dogmatist, he 'will have nothing to say against anyone who
asserts the opposite' (*M* VIII 26).

The idea is simple and effective. If you advance P as an hypothesis, then by definition you neither argue for P nor allege anything at all in its favour – your utterance of P is a bare assertion. But
then someone else hypothesizes that P*. There is nothing to be said
for P which cannot be said for P*, or *vice versa*. And for a
delightfully straightforward reason: there is nothing at all to be
said for P and nothing at all to be said for P*. If there were, they
would not be being hypothesized. Again, the Dogmatist cannot say
anything *against* P*. For anything said against P* would be something said in favour of P. But nothing is said in favour of P, since P is
hypothesized.

One general Pyrrhonian strategy consists in the setting up of
equipollent oppositions: the sceptic takes two incompatible views
and shows that they are ἰσοσθενή, equally strong, in that the
arguments for the one exactly match the arguments for the other.
Hence suspension of judgement. Now the hypothetical mode is – as
the mathematicians put it – a 'limiting case' of this strategy. The
two hypotheses, P and P*, are ἰσοσθενή, equipollent or equally
strong, in that they are supported by exactly matching arguments.
And they are supported by exactly matching arguments because
they are not – and cannot be – supported by any arguments at all.

(Here – to revert briefly to an earlier matter – we can see how the
hypothetical mode is more closely connected to ἐποχή than is
either the regressive mode or the reciprocal mode. Like them, the
hypothetical mode will usually (but not always) work in collaboration with other modes; unlike them, there is something about its
own specific character which determines the type of work it does

and its horsepower. For it is because hypothesizing is *hypothesizing* – and not because it is a sort of bad argument – that it induces or helps to induce suspension of judgement. The regressive mode and the reciprocal mode help to produce scepticism insofar as regressive arguments and reciprocal arguments are *bad* arguments. The hypothetical mode serves the sceptic in virtue of the special nature of hypothesizing.)

Now if the Dogmatists try to choose among putative and rival hypotheses, they must surely offer some reasons for rejecting their opponents' P* and for preferring their own P. But in that case, as *M* III 12 implicitly remarks, they will be abandoning the hypothetical method and seeking instead for proofs or arguments. For insofar as they produce reasons for P and against P*, to that extent they are no longer treating P as an hypothesis, and they cannot claim that it is a first principle. The hypothetical mode of the Pyrrhonists has forced them to abandon the hypothetical method.

In all this the Pyrrhonist has, or so I think, a very plausible case; and in it lies the strength of the hypothetical mode and of Sextus' first argument against the hypothetical method. But the Dogmatists are not yet dead, nor has their hypothetical method been finally exploded. In the next chapter I shall consider this matter further. Here I conclude by casting an eye over the remaining part of Sextus' description of the hypothetical mode, viz. his reply to the Dogmatists' attempt to save their method.

The Dogmatists had, Sextus says, a customary reply to the hypothetical mode:

> In reply, they habitually say that a warrant that the hypothesis is strong (ἐρρῶσθαι) can be found in the fact that what is inferred from the hypothetical assumptions is found to be true – for if what follows from them is sound, then the assumptions from which the conclusions follow are also true and indisputable. (*M* VIII 375; cf. *M* III 14).

An hypothesis is thus tested by its consequences: we may prefer P to P* provided that the consequences of P are true and the consequences of P* false.

This idea (which finds its origins in Plato's *Phaedo*) is not obviously silly. Modern epistemologists may see in it something akin to the procedure known as 'inference to the best explanation'. We may – it is said – rationally choose among competing hypotheses by selecting the hypothesis which best explains the phenomena. For example, we may prefer a Copernican to a Ptolemaic theory of the solar system just because the Copernican theory offers a better explanation of the observed celestial phenomena. The two theories may be regarded as conflicting hypotheses. Each has certain consequences or implications for the phenomena; and we shall rationally choose the theory or hypothesis with the truer implications. Thus a theory – an hypothesis – is properly tested by its consequences.[16]

Sextus raises two objections (*M* VIII 376–8; *M* III 14–17). His second objection accuses the Dogmatists of bad logic; for he represents them as arguing in favour of the hypothesis that P_1 by *inferring* it from two premisses, viz. P_2 and the conditional 'If P_1, then P_2'. (They consider the consequences of P_1, and if the consequences are true, they infer that the hypothesis is true. Hence they commit the fallacy of 'affirming the consequent'.) But this is *ignoratio elenchi* on Sextus' part. For the Dogmatists do not – or need not – hold that the truth of the hypothesis can be *inferred* from the truth of its consequences. Rather they hold – or they should hold – that an hypothesis may be *confirmed* or given strength (ἐρρῶσθαι) by the truth of its consequences. It is one thing to hold that P_1 follows deductively from P_2 (together with 'If P_1, then P_2'), another to hold that P_1 is confirmed or corroborated by P_2. The matter is no doubt less simple than Sextus' Dogmatists make it appear, and there may be serious logical objections to their procedure; but they are surely not guilty of the logical howler which Sextus ascribes to them.

Sextus' first objection is epistemological rather than logical. The objection is simply this: How can we discover whether or not the consequences of a given hypothesis are true? If we could discover that P_2, say, was true, then perhaps we might allow the hypothesis

---

16 For a critical account of 'inference to the best explanation' see Nancy Cartwright, *How the Laws of Physics Lie* (Oxford, 1983), pp.4–18. I do not of course mean that the ancient Dogmatists discovered this method of inference: their response to the hypothetical mode is similar to, but not identical with, the method.

to be thereby confirmed or given strength. But the Dogmatists may not sunnily assume that we can discover the truth or falsity of the consequences of the hypothesis.

Sextus is not merely wheeling in the old Pyrrhonian machine; he is not merely calling on general sceptical conclusions ('We can never discover the truth') and then applying them specifically to the consequences of the hypothesis. Rather, his argument is directed specifically at the status of P₂ as the consequence of *an hypothesis*. The Aristotelian hypotheses are ἀρχαί. They are epistemologically prior to their consequences. They are epistemological primitives. The Dogmatists adduce them in order to explain how we can properly warrant beliefs or even claim knowledge. We may claim (they say) to know that P₂ in so far as we can derive it from some known ἀρχή or ὑπόθεσις; and we can claim (they add) to know the ἀρχή or ὑπόθεσις in virtue of itself or directly – we may *simply* hypothesize it.

Now if the Dogmatists go on to make the further claim that the hypotheses may be chosen for their consequences, the whole epistemological order of things is overturned. Instead of resting our claim that P₂ on our claim that P₁, we go the other way about: P₁ is justifiably hypothesized because it yields P₂, which we may, properly and independently, claim to know. There is a crucial difference here between the old hypothetical method and the modern method of inference to the best explanation. The modern method is a method for producing explanations. It takes the phenomena as given and it seeks to justify a theory or hypothesis which will then explain the phenomena. The ancient method is a method for justifying or establishing the consequences of an hypothesis. It takes the axioms – the hypotheses – as given and then seeks to justify the theorems. Thus if the Dogmatists do attempt to select hypotheses by way of their consequences, they suffer an epistemological *bouleversement*. And one thing is pretty plain: by this *bouleversement* they destroy the hypothetical character of their hypotheses, and they change totally the nature – and hence the epistemological appeal – of the hypothetical method.

Should we conclude that Sextus successfully resists the Dogmatists' reply to the hypothetical mode? Yes and no. Yes: for he does, I believe, show that their reply involves a substantial change to the hypothetical method – so great a change that the whole character of hypotheses and their epistemological role is altered. No: for Sextus does not show that a new form of hypothesis in a new role may not do epistemological duty. Sextus may be right in what he says, but more remains to be said. And that, too, will be a subject of the next, and final, chapter.

5

The sceptic's net

In the four preceding chapters I have discussed four Pyrrhonian 'modes of scepticism', four general argument-forms by which the Pyrrhonists thought that suspension of judgement might be induced. I have discussed the modes as though they were independent argument-forms, each by itself capable – in certain contexts – of introducing scepticism. And these modes were often so used by Sextus.

My discussion has left many loose ends, some of which I shall tie up in this last chapter. In addition, the previous chapters have deliberately ignored one important fact about the Agrippan modes; for, as I have said, the Four Modes I have discussed were part of a set or group of modes: they are four of the Five Modes of Agrippa. The fifth Agrippan mode is the mode of relativity, the mode ἀπὸ τοῦ πρός τι. It is a strange beast, and it poses numerous and interesting problems; but it belongs – or so I think – to a different species from the other Four Modes, and I shall say nothing about it here.[1] Rather, I want to consider some ways in which the Agrippan modes may form a sceptical system; in particular, I want to consider what I shall call the Pyrrhonian net, a net in which the sceptical gladiators thought they could entangle their Dogmatic opponents.

Although Sextus often uses the Agrippan modes independently of one another, he more often uses them in groups – in pairs or in triplets. And it is plain that they were considered to have some sort of systematic interrelationship. This is hinted at in Sextus' initial characterization of the modes; for he says that the hypothetical

---

1 For some discussion see Julia Annas and Jonathan Barnes, *The Modes of Scepticism* (Cambridge, 1985), Chapter 11.

mode is used 'when the Dogmatists are thrown back *ad infinitum*', i.e. when they are threatened by the mode of regression (*PH* I 168). And after this initial characterization he remarks that 'every matter of enquiry can be brought under these modes' (I 169) and proceeds to construct a system involving all Five Modes (I 170–7).

The System of Five Modes – the system which Sextus presents, and which is perhaps his own invention[2] – is a curious thing: it is positively rococo in its complexity, yet it possesses neither aesthetic elegance nor philosophical cohesion. Nor are the Agrippan modes ever again used in this systematic fashion in Sextus' writings.

I shall not trouble to expound the Sextan system. In any case, it is easy enough to construct a modified version of the system which involves only the four Agrippan argument-forms I have discussed. The System of Four Modes works in the following fashion: take any problem ?Q. Suppose that there are (at least) two incompatible solutions to it, P and P*. Now, by the διαφωνία mode we shall be aware that there is disagreement over ?Q, some opting for P and others for P*. Hence if we are to answer the problem ?Q we must decide or resolve the διαφωνία. Suppose we think that P is in fact the correct answer to ?Q. Can we warrant or justify this thought?

At the outset we seem to have two possible procedures: we might simply *affirm* P without more ado; or we might offer some reason in support of P. If we follow the first procedure and simply affirm P, then the sceptic will adduce the hypothetical mode – to our bare assertion of P he will oppose the bare assertion of P*, and we shall be stymied. Hence we must follow the second procedure. Let us then advance reason R_1 in support of P. Now, by διαφωνία R_1 will be contested, and we must somehow decide in its favour. We cannot – by the hypothetical mode – merely assert it. Therefore we must produce some reason in favour of R_1. Let that be R_2. Well, either R_2 is identical with P or it is a new idea. If it is identical with P, then we are brought to scepticism by the reciprocal mode. (For we are supporting P by R_1 and R_1 by P.) If R_2 is new, then it will be subject to dispute. We cannot resolve the dispute by merely asserting R_2 (the hypothetical mode forbids this easy option). Hence we

---

2 Note the first person (ὑποδείξομεν) at the start of the system (I 169) as opposed to the third person (παραδιδόασι) at the start of the description (I 164). But this point is less than probative.

move on to R_3. If R_3 is not a new idea (if it is identical with P or with R_1), then the reciprocal mode is brought up. If it is new, then the hypothetical mode obliges us to produce a further reason, R_4. And in this way, by repeated application of διαφωνία, hypothesis and reciprocity, we are led into an infinite regression, R_4 being supported by R_5, R_5 by R_6; and so on without end. But this endless path is forbidden by the mode of regression.

(Note that when the reciprocity mode is used in this or in any other systematic fashion, it must be construed so as to outlaw any form of circular argumentation. Suppose that R_4 is not a new idea: if it is identical with R_2, then we have a simple case of reciprocity in the narrow sense of the word; but if R_4 is identical with R_1 or with P, then we have a circularity rather than a reciprocity. I shall continue to talk in this chapter of the reciprocal mode – it would be confusing to change the established nomenclature. But the reader should bear in mind that the arguments which the 'reciprocal' mode is intended to exclude may well be circularities rather than true reciprocities.)

The System of Four Modes is my own invention in the sense that no ancient text explicitly describes it. But it has some claim to historical reality; for it is implicitly employed by Sextus in several passages. The briefest and clearest is this:

> If the disagreement about the criterion is to be decided, then we must have an agreed criterion by which to judge it; and if we are to have an agreed criterion, we must first decide the disagreement about the criterion. Thus the argument falls into the reciprocal mode, and the search for a criterion reaches an impasse. For we shall not allow them to assume a criterion by hypothesis; and if they want to judge a criterion by a criterion, we shall throw them back *ad infinitum*.
>
> (*PH* II 20)

Sextus does not exactly follow the map of argument I sketched out, and his invocation of the reciprocal mode is flawed. (It is a case of what I have called generic reciprocity, not of genuine reciprocity.) But he does intend to use the four modes which the System invokes; and it is plain that his brief argument can plausibly be expanded and organized by way of the System of Four Modes.

There is an oddity about the Four Modes: one of them,

διαφωνία, seems to perform a different function from the other three. Whenever the hypothetical mode or the mode of regression or the reciprocity mode is deployed, the result is ἐποχή – a line of thought is blocked or shown to lead only to suspension of judgement. But διαφωνία does not block any line of thought – it does not itself induce ἐποχή. Then what *is* its function?

In my first chapter I mentioned the possibility that the existence of διαφωνία should be regarded as a *necessary* condition for ἐποχή: if an opinion is not disputed, we shall not suspend judgement over it. I urged both that there was no good textual evidence for ascribing this idea to the Pyrrhonists, and that the idea is philosophically untenable – for it is simply false that suspension of judgement requires disagreement. Hence in the Four Modes we should not regard διαφωνία as supplying an epistemologically necessary condition for the generation of scepticism. Rather, it should be thought of as a psychologically useful aid to the sceptic. If there is no disagreement at all on some issue, then you might well – if erroneously – imagine that there was no room or reason for doubt, that you were justified in assenting to the opinion insofar as there was no dissentient voice. Hence the observation of disagreement is pertinent to Pyrrhonism: it draws attention to the fact that assent should not be given without ado – doubts *might* be raised because doubts *have* been raised. This psychological use of disagreement is, I think, an important feature of Sextus' writings. After all, he is concerned (or he pretends to be concerned) to lead us to scepticism; and anything which will entice us, or show us reason to be enticed, is useful to him.

That said, we might think to dismiss διαφωνία from further discussion. Its role as an independent purveyor of scepticism I have already investigated: in the System of Four Modes it has no philosophically interesting role to play.

And so we might think to develop a system of three modes. Now there is in fact a system of three modes in Sextus. But it has a misleading nomenclature – and it does not contain the particular three modes we want to be left with. Having dealt with the Five Modes, Sextus turns briefly to what he calls 'two other modes of suspension' (1 178). The Two Modes form a system, and I am inclined to think that this system comes from Agrippa himself.[3] But the System of Two Modes introduces neither new modes nor two modes. Rather, at *PH* I 178–9, Sextus outlines a way in which three of the familiar Five Modes may be deployed in concert. The three modes are διαφωνία, regression and reciprocity; and by their joint application we are supposed to see that any issue whatsoever must lead to scepticism and ἐποχή.

> Since everything which is known is thought to be known either from itself or from something else, they point out that things are known neither from themselves nor from anything else, and so think to introduce perplexity about everything. That nothing is known from itself is clear, they say, from the disagreements among the natural scientists, which have, I suppose, concerned every matter, whether an object of perception or an object of thought, and which are undecided; for we cannot use either an object of perception or an object of thought as a criterion inasmuch as anything we might take will be a matter of disagreement and hence without warranty. And for this reason they do not allow that anything can be known from anything else. For if that from which something is known must always itself be known from something else, they fall either into the reciprocal or into the regressive mode. And should you wish to assume something as known from itself, so that something else can be known from it, then you are blocked by the fact that nothing is known from itself (for the reasons I have given).   (*PH* I 178–9)

The System of 'Two' Modes may be shown by means of a diagram. Start with the Dogmatist's claim – with *any* claim – at the top of the diagram. The possible paths which the Dogmatist may take are marked by the downward diagonal lines. When an item

---

3 Sextus says 'They also hand down (παραδιδόασι)' the Two Modes (*PH* I 178). The subject of παραδιδόασι is surely 'the more recent sceptics', who are referred to in I 177 as the begetters of the Five Modes. Strictly speaking, it does not follow that the *same* more recent sceptics produced the Two Modes; but it seems to me that the natural and obvious way of reading Sextus' text has him ascribing the same paternity to the Two as to the Five Modes. Since Agrippa is father of the Five, he is also father of the Two. (This is an unorthodox, though not a novel, view. Most scholars, for no good reason, assume that the Two Modes must derive from an author *later* than Agrippa.)

appears in the diagram for the first time, it is called 'new'; other-wise it is old. When a diagonal is blocked by horizontal bars ($= = = = =$), the meaning is that, so far as this line of argument goes, the Dogmatist must suspend judgement. Since all possible paths in the diagram are eventually blocked by horizontal bars, the Dogmatist must suspend judgement in all cases (see diagram 1).

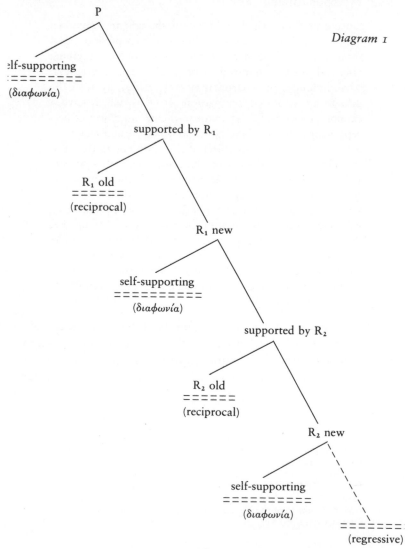

Diagram 1

Here διαφωνία has, after all, a function in a systematic presentation of the Agrippan modes. (As he says, Sextus has *undecided* disagreement in mind.) The thought is this: any proposition which you may claim to know 'from itself' – any claim which is allegedly self-supporting – will be subject to disagreement; and the disagreement will be undecided, since we have no agreed decision procedure by which to decide it.

Thus the place of διαφωνία in the System of 'Two' Modes depends on the argument which I discussed at the end of the first chapter. Although that argument is interesting, I do not want to discuss it again; and although the 'Two' Modes form an interesting system, they ignore the hypothetical mode – which, as I have said, is a mode of the first importance to the Pyrrhonists. I therefore propose to replace the 'Two' Modes by what I shall call the System of Three Modes. The new system is in fact isomorphic with the System of 'Two' Modes: all that happens is that the position of διαφωνία in the 'Two' Modes is taken in the Three by the hypothetical mode. Thus the mode of disagreement finally departs from these pages. I do not deny its interest or its sceptical importance. But I have no more to say about it; and it will – I hope – be plain that the System of Three Modes is superior to the System of 'Two'.

The Three Modes work like this. Suppose you are considering the claim that P. Then either (1) the claim is merely asserted, or else (2) it is supported. If (1), then the hypothetical mode applies. If (2), then P rests on some reason or set of reasons, R_1. Either (2a) R_1 is an 'old' item, i.e. (in this case) it is the same as P, or else (2b) it is a new item. If (2a), then the reciprocal mode applies. If (2b), then either (2bi) R_1 is merely asserted or (2bii) R_1 is supported. If (2bi), then the hypothetical mode applies. And so on . . . until the regressive mode is invoked.

Again, a diagram will make things plainer. The new diagram is constructed on the lines of the old (see diagram 2). This diagram, and the System of Three Modes, represents – or so I think – the philosophical core of Agrippan scepticism; and it conveys what is epistemologically most important and most challenging about this aspect of ancient Pyrrhonism.

The Three Modes, like the Four, are in a sense my own invention. But they too have an historical reality of sorts. And I shall

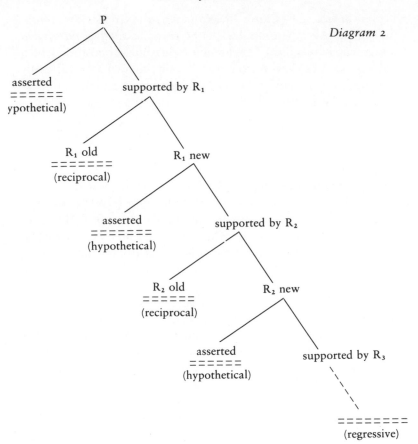

Diagram 2

indulge in a brief historical comment before I turn to the fundamental philosophical issues which the Three Modes raise.

I have already referred more than once to the passage in Aristotle's *Posterior Analytics* where he adverts to epistemological regressions and to circular proofs. In that passage, *APst* A 3, Aristotle is concerned with the general possibility of knowledge (or rather, of 'scientific' knowledge, of ἐπιστήμη), and hence he is implicitly concerned with scepticism.[4] He considers the suggestion

4 For a detailed analysis of *APst* A 3 see Jonathan Barnes, *Aristotle's Posterior Analytics* (Oxford, 1976), pp.106–12.

that any known proposition must be based on some other known proposition; that if I know that P, then I must base my knowledge on knowledge of some R_i. In that case, of two things one. Either every item will be supported by a new item, and an infinite chain of knowledge will be generated. But, according to Aristotle, such infinite epistemological sequences are impossible. Or else at some point in the process an old item will be reintroduced, and we shall have a circular proof. But, according to Aristotle, there are insurmountable objections to circular proofs.

Hence, Aristotle concludes, we must reject the suggestion that every known proposition must be based on some other known proposition – if we are to have any knowledge at all. In some cases we may properly claim knowledge even though we do not base the claim on any further claim.

Thus Aristotle rejects infinite epistemological regressions and implicitly accepts the Pyrrhonist's regressive mode. He rejects circular reasoning and implicitly accepts the Pyrrhonist's reciprocal mode. But he rejects scepticism, and explicitly supposes that at some point in the argument a 'new' R_i may, with reason and justification, be simply asserted. Thus he implicitly rejects the Pyrrhonist's hypothetical mode or else implicitly requires that there must be some *via media* between hypothesizing and supporting, between producing a bare assertion and offering supporting reasons.

The connexion between *APst* A 3 and the Agrippan modes has often been noticed.[5] There is the closest thematic similarity – the diagram by which I illustrated the System of Three Modes (or the System of 'Two' Modes) will equally serve in an elucidation of Aristotle's argument. Moreover, there are linguistic parallels between Aristotle's text and Sextus' exposition of Agrippa's modes. The similarities are striking, and they can hardly be accidental. There must be some historical link between Aristotle and Agrippa. Now we know that there was a renascence of interest in Aristotelianism towards the end of the first century BC.[6] We might

5 See e.g. A.A. Long, 'Aristotle and the History of Greek Scepticism', in D.J. O'Meara (ed.), *Studies in Aristotle* (Washington DC, 1981).
6 See most recently H.B. Gottschalk, 'Aristotelian Philosophy in the Roman World from the time of Cicero to the end of the second century AD', in W. Haase (ed.), *Aufstieg und Niedergang der Römischen Welt* II 36.2 (Berlin, 1987).

guess that Agrippa, who lived in roughly this period, read, or learned about, the *Posterior Analytics*; that he was impressed by Aristotle's discussion in A 3; and that he saw how it could be adapted to Pyrrhonian ends. He had only to agree with Aristotle in his treatment of regression and reciprocity while rejecting Aristotle's own way of escaping from scepticism. This rejection he could have secured in either of two ways: by appealing to the notion of διαφωνία, already dear to the Pyrrhonists, and thereby constructing the System of 'Two' Modes; or by adducing the hypothetical mode, familiar from sceptical arguments against the hypothetical method of the geometers, and thereby constructing the System of Three Modes. Thus Agrippa's modes – or their central philosophical core – will have derived historically from the *Posterior Analytics*. Aristotle was unknowingly the great-grandfather of the sturdiest child the sceptics ever produced.

The story, as I have sketched it, requires – and can be given – further elaboration and refinement. But it must remain to some extent a fantasy; for although there is no evidence against it, and although *some* such history is surely needed to account for the facts, there is no evidence for any particular or detailed version of the historical tale. Let us hope that new discoveries – perhaps in the excavations at Herculaneum – may eventually produce the telling document. Until then, we shall be prudent if, while believing that Aristotle somehow influenced Agrippa, we refrain from speculating about the exact way in which the influence was exerted.

I turn therefore from historical to philosophical speculation. How might a Dogmatist, ancient or modern, evade the Pyrrhonian cast? Or how might he wriggle out of the net in which the Three Modes tangle him?

As far as I am aware, no philosopher has seriously supposed that the mode of regression should be rejected, or that a Dogmatic epistemology could be founded on infinite sequences of beliefs. The reciprocal mode has been questioned, implicitly, by some philosophers both ancient and modern. But the ancient patrons of circularity have left us nothing of constructive interest. In point of fact, nearly all ancient and most modern Dogmatists have in effect followed Aristotle. That is to say, they have attempted either to reject the hypothetical mode or to find a *via media* between bare assertion and rational support. (And I am inclined to think that there is not a genuine disjunction here: there are not two distinct things which different epistemologists have attempted to do; rather, their attempts to escape the net may – or so I suggest – be described indifferently as rejections of the hypothetical mode or as inventions of a *via media*.)

The Aristotelians, then, try to characterize a class of propositions which may with propriety be hypothesized. There are some propositions, they urge, which we may reasonably accept as hypotheses – because in their case either bare assertion is admissible or else hypothesizing is something other than bare assertion. These propositions will then form the basis of our belief systems; they will, in a standard metaphor, constitute the foundations of our knowledge. (The metaphor is an ancient one.[7] The moderns have used it in subtly different ways, and I do not pretend that my use of it here is the only permissible or fruitful use.) Thus Aristotelians offer a 'foundationalist' epistemology. Such an epistemology divides our items of knowledge or our justified beliefs into two classes: some items of knowledge – some justified beliefs – are fundamental or basic; the remainder are dependent or derivative. An item is dependent or derivative just in case it derives its epistemic status – its status as an item known or justifiably believed – from some other item (or set of items) which is known or justifiably believed. An item is fundamental or basic just in case it is known or justifiably believed and yet does not derive this epistemic status from any other item which is known or justifiably believed.

More formally, we may offer the following schema as an abstract and general representation of a foundationalist epistemology.

> x knows or justifiably believes that P just in case
> *either* (i) there is some set of propositions Π such that (a) every member of Π is known or justifiably believed by x, and (b) P stands in an appropriate epistemic relation to the members of Π;
> *or else* (ii) P belongs to the class β of basic beliefs.

As I have said, almost all Dogmatists have been foundationalists. Hence almost all have subscribed to one instance or another of this abstract schema.

7 See in Sextus *PH* II 84; *M* VII 216; IX 2; *M* III 12 (above, p. 106); V 50.

I say 'almost all' rather than 'all'; for 'coherence' theories of knowledge or justification are normally taken – by their proponents and by their opponents – to entail a denial of foundationalism. A coherence theory, it is said, recognizes no basic items of knowledge: every item owes its epistemic status to its relationship to other items. And in that case, coherence theorists, as I hinted in an earlier chapter, must implicitly reject the reciprocal mode.

But there is, I think, another way of construing the strategy of coherentism: coherence theories can be interpreted as special cases of foundationalism. Nothing much turns on this odd claim; but it does, I think, permit us to consider versions of coherentism which would otherwise seem to be ruled out of court. What I have in mind is this. A coherence theorist could accept the foundationalist schema; and he could use the notion of coherence not to explain non-basic knowledge, but to determine the basic category β. He might perhaps say something like this:

> P belongs to β just in case the degree of coherence within β is greater if it includes P than if it excludes P.

Thus we know P by virtue of coherence insofar as P satisfies clause (ii) of the particular coherentist version of the foundationalist schema. What of clause (i) of the schema? A coherentist *may* hold – and perhaps all actual coherentists have in effect held – that clause (i) determines an empty set: all knowledge is 'basic' knowledge. (The schema remains apt. Its disjunctive condition will be verified only by the verification of the second disjunct – the first disjunct will be idle. But that is no objection.) Yet, so far as I can see, a coherentist need not hold that clause (i) determines an empty set. For, while maintaining that coherence is what fixes our basic beliefs, he could well allow that some beliefs get their justification in a derivative fashion. (In terms of the model or analogy in Chapter 3: there may be some flag-poles to which no rope is tied by its red end.) Whether or not this is possible will depend on the precise form which the coherence theory takes. But in principle it seems that one could develop a coherentism which included non-basic items. If that is true, then my suggestion that coherentism is a special case of foundationalism is necessary. And if it is not true, my proposal is pointless – but harmlessly so.

However that may be, the foundationalist schema certainly embraces either all or almost all Dogmatic epistemologies. In introducing the schema here, I am not imposing a modern conception on the ancient texts. On the contrary, the ancients were aware of the general structure of the schema. The earliest clear example of it is to be found in Plato's *Theaetetus* (201D–202C). More to the present point, it is this schema which determines the general strategy of Sextus' attack on Dogmatic epistemology in *PH* II and *M* VII–VIII. The distinction between the two classes of items in the schema is represented in Sextus by the ancient distinction between on the one hand signs (σημεῖα) and proofs (ἀποδείξεις) and on the other criteria (κριτήρια). For we may say – with only slight simplification – that items are known by signs or proofs just in case they are items of dependent or derivative knowledge, and that items are known by a criterion just in case they are basic or fundamental items of knowledge.[8] And in *PH* II and *M* VII–VIII Sextus attacks in turn the possibility of providing a criterion of truth and the possibility of providing a theory of signs.

> Since the Dogmatists think that what is evident is known directly by way of some criterion and that what is unclear is tracked down by way of signs and proofs by inference from what is evident, let us consider in order, first, whether there is any criterion for those items which directly impress the senses or the intellect, and then whether there is any way of producing signs or proofs of what is unclear. (*M* VII 25)

In other words, Sextus proposes to tackle in turn the possibility of basic knowledge and the possibility of derivative knowledge.

Here we are concerned with basic or fundamental items, and with the criterion of truth. Sextus' attack on the criterion is a characteristic mish-mash of arguments: some of them are painfully

---

8 On the concept of the criterion see especially Gisela Striker, Κριτήριον τῆς ᾿Αληθείας (Göttingen, 1974); and, most recently, the essays collected in Pamela Huby and Gordon Neal (edd.), *The Criterion of Truth* (Liverpool, 1989). Both historically and philosophically the matter is far more complex than my simple remarks here and later may suggest, but in the present context the complexities are unimportant. (I should perhaps note that the ancient use of the word 'criterion' is quite different from the Wittgensteinian use with which modern philosophers are more familiar.)

feeble, some seem merely frivolous, a few are profound and challenging.[9] I touched on one of these arguments in the first chapter.
Here, rather than trace the discussion under Sextus' guidance, I
shall follow a different path.

The question concerns basic beliefs, members of the class β.
Different epistemologists have determined membership of this
class in different ways: perhaps it contains self-explanatory propositions, or self-evident propositions, or propositions which are
directly given in perception, or records of sense-data, or analytical
truths, or innate beliefs, or propositions which we are naturally
determined to accept, or propositions which form the structure and
framework of our human or social 'form of life'. And so on.
Different epistemologies offer different sorts of basic beliefs, and
these differences import different particular questions and different particular problems. But from the Pyrrhonian point of view,
they all face one common and daunting objection: how can it be
that membership of β, whatever may determine it, is enough to
generate knowledge or to justify belief?

For the Dogmatist, of whatever particular persuasion, affirms
that P, and takes his affirmation to be legitimate insofar as P is a
member of β. And the sceptic retorts as follows: 'You affirm that P.
But you offer nothing in support of P – your claim is an hypothesis
or bare assertion. Why then should I accept it? Or come to that,
why should *you* accept it? Since P is putatively basic, you may not
offer any argument or reason in its support. But if you offer – if you
can offer – nothing in its support, then it is surely worthless. Or
rather, it is worth exactly as much and as little as any other
incompatible claim.' (This line of reflection is of course no more
than a rehearsal of the hypothetical mode.)

Now it may seem quite obvious that the Dogmatists have an easy
reply to this sceptical retort. For, as I said in the previous chapter,
they claim to be able to *choose* among putative hypotheses: they do
not offer *any* proposition as a suitable hypothesis. The sceptics
urge that the Dogmatists might as well offer P* as P. But the

9 See A.A. Long, 'Sextus Empiricus on the Criterion of Truth', *Bulletin
    of the Institute of Classical Studies* 25, 1978, 35–49; Jacques
    Brunschwig, 'Sextus Empiricus on the *kriterion*: the Skeptic as
    Conceptual Legatee', in J.M. Dillon and A.A. Long (edd.), *The
    Question of 'Eclecticism'* (Berkeley, 1988).

Dogmatists are not at all prepared to accept this suggestion. And we can now see exactly how they will reject it: they will say that they are entitled to hypothesize P (rather than P*) precisely because P (and not P*) belongs to β. If P belongs to β, then P* does not belong to β. For whatever the composition of β, it will contain only true propositions. Hence if P is in β, then neither P* nor any other 'opposite' of P can be in β. Thus the Dogmatists *do* have a reason for advancing P rather than P*. They advance P because P is in β. They do not advance P*, because P* is not in β. When they hypothesize P, their claim may or may not still count as a 'bare assertion' (they do not really care); but it is certainly not arbitrarily made or unwarrantably advanced – its warranty is found in its membership of β.

But to this ready reply by the Dogmatists, the Pyrrhonists once again have a ready response. For the Dogmatists surely now appear to be offering an *argument* in favour of P. They appear to be justifying their claim that P by reference to the fact that P is a member of β. They seem, in other words, to be producing the following little piece of reasoning.

(1) P is in β
(2) Therefore, P

For example:

(1*) It is directly given in perception that honey is sweet
(2*) Therefore, honey is sweet

– as an Epicurean might have argued. Now this argument may be a perfectly decent argument in itself. But – or so the Pyrrhonist will evidently urge – it is not an argument which the Dogmatists may use at this point in their reasoning. For it derives P from some other proposition, viz. the proposition that P is in β, and insofar as it does so, it no longer takes P itself as a basic proposition.

The sceptic is not arguing that the Dogmatists' position is incoherent or paradoxical. He is not arguing, for example, that if P is derived from proposition (1), then P cannot itself be a member of β because in that case the proposition that P is a member of β will be a member of β. That might sound neatly paradoxical – but it would be an unreal paradox. The sceptic's point is simpler and sounder than that: if P is derived from anything at all, and hence in particular, if it is derived from the proposition that P is in β, then it is not a member of β.

Of course, if a Dogmatist uses a piece of reasoning of this sort, if, say, he offers (1*) in support of (2*), then the sceptic can no longer object, by the hypothetical mode, that his claim – the claim, say, that (2*) is true – is a bare assertion. But this does not constitute an answer to the sceptic: it merely displaces the sceptic's challenge. For – and evidently – he will now turn his attention to (1*). Is *that* proposition supported or not? If it is supported, then reciprocity and regression threaten and the Dogmatist has in effect abandoned his foundationalism, at least *pro tempore*. But if (1*) is not supported, then why should we accept it – and why should the Dogmatist accept it – rather than an 'opposite' proposition, say the proposition that P* is in β? In short, if the Dogmatist protects (2*) from the hypothetical mode by the shield of (1*), he leaves (1*) to face the sceptic's attack, unarmed and armourless. Nothing whatsoever has been accomplished.

Is the Pyrrhonist now triumphant? No. There is a further step in the dialectical dance. It is relatively subtle.

Let us take a standard Dogmatic argument. Dogmatists believed that there are invisible pores in our skin, and their reason for believing so was that we sweat.[10] According to them, we have derivative knowledge that there are invisible pores in the skin and (let us suppose) direct knowledge that we sweat. Thus they claim to warrant their belief that there are pores by way of the following argument:

> (A) We sweat
> Therefore, there are invisible pores in our skin

And they claim that we sweat without offering any reason or argument.

The last Pyrrhonist manoeuvre in effect forced the Dogmatists to *argue* for the claim that we sweat, and to argue for it as follows.

> (B) It is immediately observable that we sweat
> Therefore, we sweat

10 See *PH* II 98, 140, 142; *M* VIII 306, 309; cf. Diogenes Laertius, IX 89 (quoted above, p.59), and note that the first of the three 'hypotheses' of the physician Asclepiades (above, p.96) affirms the existence of imperceptible pores (*M* III 5).

For the Dogmatists averred that they were justified in claiming that we sweat because it is a basic truth that we sweat – and the Pyrrhonists took this to amount to the suggestion that the Dogmatists argue for their basic belief from the premiss that it *is* a basic belief.

But since, according to the Pyrrhonists, argument (B) is on a par with argument (A), the Dogmatist will now be abandoning any claim to basic knowledge: just as argument (A) makes the invisible pores an item of derivative knowledge, so argument (B) in effect treats our sweating as a derivative and not a basic item of knowledge.

Now it is plain that argument (B) is not in all respects like argument (A), and it is reasonable to wonder whether the differences may not be to the advantage of the Dogmatist. In particular, in (A) the premiss gives *evidence* for the conclusion – our sweating is, as the Dogmatists said, a sign of the existence of pores. In (B), on the other hand, the premiss is not evidential in this way: that sweating is immediately observed is not *evidence* – it is not a sign – that sweating takes place. Premiss and conclusion are differently related in (A) and in (B).

The point may emerge more clearly if we adduce a third argument, namely:

(C) The existence of invisible pores can be proved from the fact that we sweat
   Therefore, there are invisible pores

Argument (C) has the same conclusion as argument (A); but in other respects it is parallel to argument (B). For in (C), as in (B), the premiss does not express evidence or a sign for the conclusion – the epistemological relation is a different one. Argument (C) is valid; and (let us grant) its premiss is true. But it is a different sort of argument from argument (A). And it is argument (A), not argument (C), on which the Dogmatist bases his claim that there are invisible pores.

Argument (B), which the Pyrrhonists foisted upon the Dogmatists, is parallel to (C) and not to (A). This is clear. And it gives us the means to produce a Dogmatic reply to the sceptic's latest objection.

The reply runs like this. If P is a non-basic justified belief, then there will be an argument like argument (A) associated with it; and this argument will be precisely what gives support to the belief or justifies the claim that P. In addition, there will be an argument parallel to argument (C). This argument, too, will be *sound*; but it is an argument quite distinct from argument (A), and it does not provide *support* for the belief or justify the claim that P. Now suppose that P is a basic belief. Here there will be no argument at all corresponding to (A): there cannot be, for if there were, P would not be a basic belief. Since there is no argument for P corresponding to argument (A), the claim is indeed unsupported, and to that extent and in that sense it is a bare assertion or a naked hypothesis. But there is an argument – a sound argument – associated with P, namely an argument parallel to argument (B). Since (B) does not correspond to (A), the existence of (B) does not show that P is after all supported and so non-basic. But since (B) exists, and corresponds to (C), its existence does show something about P: in fact, it shows that we are justified or warranted in claiming that P, and that we are justified or warranted precisely because (B) is a good argument. (Note how argument (B) distinguishes P from any of its 'opposites'. No argument similar to (B) will be available for the 'opposites' of P; for any such argument would be unsound inasmuch as any opposite of P would be false.)

Thus the Dogmatists may, after all, welcome argument (B). It does indeed enable them to escape from the hypothetical mode. But it does not mean that P loses its status as a basic belief.

Now that may sound very clever, but it may also have the appearance of a conjuring trick. For is the Dogmatist not claiming that (B) somehow both supports and *warrants* and also does not support or *make derivative* his belief that P? How can he explain the role of argument (B) without actually turning it into a supporting argument of the objectionable sort?

Well, argument (A) represents the Dogmatist's own reasoning. He believes the premiss of (A); and because he believes the premiss he believes the conclusion. If the premiss is R_1 and the conclusion is P, then because the Dogmatist believes that R_1, he believes that P; and his belief in R_1 justifies his belief in P. Now this is not so in the case of argument (B), or in the case of (C). Here the Dogmatist does not believe the premiss. (Or rather, he *need* not believe the premiss – his epistemic attitude to the premiss does not determine his epistemic attitude to the conclusion.) He believes the conclusion; and because the premiss holds he believes the conclusion. But it is not the case that he believes that the conclusion holds because he believes that the premiss holds.

The crucial difference between (A) and (B) is this. In the case of (A) we may say:

(α) Because x believes that R_1, x believes that P.

In the case of (B), we may say:

(β) Because R_1, x believes that P.

Now the fact that in argument (B) the Dogmatist does not believe the premiss – is not *committed* to believing the premiss – shows that in this case there is nothing corresponding to (α); and hence that his belief in P is indeed properly manifested in a bare assertion or an hypothesis. (For what it is for a belief to be barely asserted is precisely for there to be no proposition of the form (α) to back it up.) But the fact that in argument (B) proposition (β) does hold shows that the belief in P is grounded and justified. (For a belief is justified provided that some appropriate truth of the form (β) is associated with it.)

In offering this account of argument (B), I am ascribing to the Dogmatists what modern philosophers have called an 'externalist' account of basic beliefs and basic knowledge. The sense of the nomenclature is this. Beliefs which are justified by virtue of proposition (α) are justified by reference to some further belief (or, more generally, some further attitude) of the believer: x's belief in P is grounded on *x's belief* in R_1. Hence the justification is 'internal' to x. Beliefs which are justified by virtue of proposition (β) are justified without reference to any further attitude of the believer: x's belief in P is grounded, not on any attitude of x towards R_1, but on *the fact* of R_1. Hence the justification is 'external' to x. Thus basic beliefs are grounded, but they are grounded on something 'external' to the believer. They are not grounded internally on other items of his belief system.

The last few pages have been abstract and non-historical. I shall end this chapter, and my discussion of the structure of Agrippan scepticism, by returning to the ancient sources. First I shall say something to indicate that it is historically appropriate to ascribe an 'externalist' form of foundationalism to the Greek Dogmatists. Then I shall ask whether the Pyrrhonists had any reply to the externalist response.

I start, obliquely, from the notion of nature and natural belief. 'All men by nature desire to know', said Aristotle in a celebrated *bon mot* (*Met* 980a1). It is echoed by Sextus: 'Man is by nature a truth-loving animal' (*M* VII 27). And gentle nature would not have given us a desire without also supplying the means to satisfy it. 'Seek and you will find, for you possess from nature dispositions towards the discovery of truth' (Epictetus, *diss* I iv 51). Or, as Galen put it, 'all men possess by nature certain first principles of reason (λογικαὶ ἀρχαί)' (*Thrasyb* v 846–7 K).

It is in Galen, in fact, that we find this theory of 'natural epistemology', as I may call it, most fully expressed. I cite three passages.[11] The first comes from his essay against the Academic sceptic, Favorinus.

> It is plainly apparent to us, even if the sophists have done their best to make it dubious, that there are natural criteria. A pair of compasses describes a circle; a rule determines lengths, just as a balance determines weights. These criteria men have constructed for themselves, starting from their natural organs and criteria, than which we possess no higher criterion more noble or more honourable. It is here, then, that we must start. For our mind tells us that it is possible to trust or to distrust natural criteria, but that it is not possible to judge them by way of anything else. For how could that by which everything else is judged be itself judged by something else?
>
> (*opt doct* I 48–9 K)

We construct artificial criteria of truth, artificial yardsticks for determining the shapes and sizes and weights of things. And we do so on the basis of our 'natural' criteria. For we possess natural criteria of truth. Just as a balance will determine, artificially, that a sack of potatoes weighs 56 pounds, so our organs will determine, naturally, that this is an apple and that a fig. (The apples and figs

---

11 For a detailed discussion of Galen's views see Michael Frede, 'On Galen's Epistemology', in V. Nutton (ed.), *Galen: Problems and Prospects* (London, 1981), reprinted in Frede's *Essays on Ancient Philosophy* (Oxford, 1987).

are Galen's examples. The potatoes are not. The comparison with artificial criteria is a commonplace in the ancient texts.)

What are these natural criteria? Galen's answer is unsurprising.

> I say that you all possess natural criteria, and in saying this I am reminding you, not teaching or proving or asserting on my own authority. And what are these criteria? Eyes in their natural state seeing visible things, ears in their natural state hearing audible things, a tongue tasting tastes, a nose for smells, the whole skin for tangible things; and in addition to these, judgement or thought or whatever you like to call it, by which we discern what follows and what conflicts, and other things of the same sort – division and collection, similarity and dissimilarity. (*PHP* v 723 K)

And a little later.

> How does Hippocrates say that the nature of things is discovered? By starting from what is greatest and easiest: greatest in utility, easiest for us to know. For nature has given us two things: the criteria themselves, and untaught trust in them. Now the criteria themselves are the sense-organs and the faculties which use these organs; and an untaught and natural trust in them is found not only in men but in the other animals too. (*PHP* v 725 K)

Place an apple before me, and my eyes will report – by nature – that there is an apple before me. If my eyes report that there is an apple before me, then – again by nature – I will trust and believe that there is an apple before me. My senses may of course err; and as the passage from *opt doct* shows, I may perversely choose to reject the evidence of my senses. None the less, if my senses are in their natural condition and if my mind is in its natural state, then I will believe that there is an apple before me just when – and just because – there is an apple before me.

This natural epistemology was not an invention of Galen's. Indeed, Galen himself claims to find it in Hippocrates (see *PHP* v 724 K) and in Plato (see *PHP* v 732 K). The theory may be discovered in Aristotle, at least in a rudimentary form.[12] We may

12 On Aristotle's epistemology see Jonathan Barnes, 'An Aristotelian Way with Scepticism', in Mohan Matthen (ed.), *Aristotle Today* (Edmonton, 1987).

care to see it in Epicurus' notion that 'Human nature was taught and compelled in many different ways by the objects themselves' (*ad Hdt* 75). But it is in Stoic and Stoic-influenced texts that the Galenian theory is most clearly and most articulately present. I shall cite a few passages from many.[13]

'Nature', according to Epictetus, 'is the strongest thing in men' (*diss* II xx 15); and mere philosophers cannot eradicate it. The Epicureans failed to remove our natural desires to be citizens and friends of one another,

> and the lazy Academics were unable to abandon or blind their own senses, even though they made every effort to do so.
>
> (*diss* II xx 20)

In general, we naturally trust our senses, and the sceptical arguments of the Academics – Epictetus might have added the Pyrrhonians – can do nothing to destroy this natural trust. For the Stoics, as for Galen, it is sense-perception which ultimately provides the criterion. For, as Sextus reports,

> nature has given us our perceptual faculty and the impressions which arise through it as, so to speak, a light for the recognition of truth, and it would be absurd to reject such a faculty and to deprive ourselves of, as it were, the light.
>
> (*M* VII 259)

And a little earlier, describing the views of the 'the more recent' Stoics, Sextus remarks that

> the criterion of truth is apprehensive impression – not without qualification, but when there is no obstacle. For this, they say, is evident and striking, and it all but grasps our hair and drags us to assent. (*M* VII 257)

Thus we have a natural faculty for discerning the truth, and we naturally yield to the promptings of the faculty. Nature illuminates the world for us. Nature grabs us and drags us to assent. Using a comparison which has already been invoked, Cicero says that

---

13 For a full discussion see Michael Frede, 'Stoics and Sceptics on Clear and Distinct Impressions', in M.F. Burnyeat (ed.), *The Skeptical Tradition* (Berkeley, 1983), reprinted in Frede's *Essays on Ancient Philosophy*.

> just as it is necessary for the balance to tip when weights are
> placed on the pan, so must the mind yield to what is evident.
>
> (*Luc* xii 38)

Thanks to nature, we may get to know the nature of things.

Again, our 'apprehensive impressions' – the experiences in virtue of which we acquire basic beliefs about the world – form a
natural class or kind of experience.

> The Stoics say that if you possess an apprehensive impression
> you hit expertly on the underlying differences among things;
> for an impression of this sort has a special character distin-
> guishing it from other impressions, just as horned snakes
> differ from other snakes. (*M* VII 252)

Just as horned snakes are a special class of snake, marked off from
other snakes by a natural and idiosyncratic feature, so apprehensive impressions are a special class of impressions, marked off by
nature from other and unreliable impressions, from dreams and
delusions and the like.

Moreover, there are some particular things which nature determines us to believe. According to Epictetus,

> it is the nature of the mind to assent to truths, to dissent from
> falsities, to suspend judgement with regard to what is unclear.
> 'What's the evidence for that?' Feel now, if you can, that it is
> night. 'Impossible,' Reject the feeling that it's day. 'Imposs-
> ible.' Feel or reject the feeling that the stars are even in
> number. 'Impossible.' (*diss* I xxviii 2–3)

If you go out in the midday sun, you will, by nature, assent to the
thought that it is day. You are naturally incapable either of denying
that it is day or even of suspending judgement on the matter.

Again, it is by a natural path that we arrive at knowledge of the
first principles of science and at basic or fundamental beliefs. For
example, the basic principle of Stoic ethics, that all animals love
themselves,

> does not admit of doubt; for it is fixed in our very nature and
> is grasped so firmly by each man's senses that if anyone tries
> to speak against it he is not heard. (Cicero, *fin* v x 27)

We believe the first principles or ἀρχαί because nature requires us to believe them. Our beliefs are naturally determined – and by a benevolent nature.

There are many difficulties and obscurities in these several texts. Moreover, it should not be assumed that they all purvey exactly the same epistemological theory. Thus according to Epictetus, we *must* assent to certain propositions; according to the 'more recent' Stoics, certain truths *almost* drag us to assent; according to Galen, we are naturally *disposed* to assent but can always choose not to. These are differences which it would be foolish to play down. But there is, none the less, a solid mass of common thought in all the texts. And at the centre lies the concept of nature.

Reference to nature is reference to natural or *causal* connexions. In saying that we are naturally inclined or dragged or compelled to assent, the Dogmatists are adverting to a causal link between the facts and our beliefs – certain states of affairs are such that, once they come to our attention, we are thereby caused to believe that they obtain. This is so, in particular, in the case of the first principles of science and of the fundamental items in our belief systems. And thus nature, or causal connectedness, provides the foundations of our knowledge.

On this view, basic beliefs – the members of class β – are what may be termed 'natural' beliefs; and natural beliefs are those beliefs towards which nature leads us, i.e. those beliefs which we are naturally caused to have by the very facts which the beliefs express. More precisely, we might offer something like this as an account of natural belief:

> x has a natural belief that P just in case
> (i) it is the fact that P which causes it to seem to x that P, and
> (ii) it is the fact that it seems to x that P which causes x to believe that P.

(It follows trivially from this that all natural beliefs are true: if something is caused by the fact that P, then it *is* a fact that P.) The account needs certain qualifications and refinements; but it is, I think, fundamentally correct as a description of the basis of Hellenistic Dogmatism.

The theory of natural belief lends itself easily to externalist epistemologies. I do not think that any ancient text advances an externalist theory expressly and self-consciously – the distinction between internalist and externalist theories was not explicitly marked by the Greeks. But for all that, it is most plausible to construe the Dogmatists as offering externalist theories, i.e. as offering theories which in fact are externalist. Thus I take the Stoics to be saying that we are justified in believing that every animal loves itself simply because this belief is impressed on us by nature: the belief is justified not because *we believe* that it is impressed on us by nature (though we may well come to believe this), but because it *is* impressed on us by nature. In general, the Stoics hold that x is justified in believing that P (where P is a basic belief) provided that

(β*) Because P is impressed on x by nature, x believes that P.

They do *not* hold that, in addition, it must be true that:

(α*) Because x believes that P is impressed on x by nature, x believes that P.

Sentences (α*) and (β*), as their labels suggest, are specifications of the sentences (α) and (β) which appeared a few pages ago. It was characteristic of an externalist epistemology that it maintained a (β)-sentence rather than an (α)-sentence. Hence the Stoics, maintaining (β*) rather than (α*), are marked as externalists.

Had the Pyrrhonists any answer to externalist epistemologies? It might well be supposed that they would reject outright any attempt to intrude nature into epistemology. Yet the supposition would be false. The Pyrrhonists cannot take blanket exception to any Dogmatic appeal to nature; for nature and natural inclinations played a leading part in their own Pyrrhonian comedy. Thus in order to explain how sceptics may live without belief, Sextus invokes 'the fourfold observation of life', the first part of which consists in 'the instruction of nature, whereby we are naturally capable of perception and thought' (*PH* I 24). Moreover, as Pyrrhonists we are invited to 'follow the phenomena';

> for we are not moved (κινούμεθα) in the same way at the present moment with regard to 'It is day' and 'It is night', or with regard to Socrates' being alive and being dead.
>
> (*M* VII 391)

The passage is strikingly similar to the Epictetan text I quoted a moment ago.

These and many similar passages raise puzzles for the interpreter of Sextus' Pyrrhonism.[14] Whatever we make of them, they show that Sextus cannot lightly brush aside the Dogmatic reliance on the causal powers of nature. If there are Pyrrhonian objections to natural epistemology, these objections must turn upon the particular form in which nature is invoked; they cannot consistently rest upon a general condemnation of appeals to nature. And in point of fact there are Sextan objections – numerous and varied, implicit and explicit – to the externalist epistemology of the Dogmatists. Here I shall rehearse only the chief and most telling line of argument.

I start with a celebrated fragment from the Presocratic philosopher Xenophanes of Colophon.

> And the clear truth no man has seen nor will anyone know
> concerning the gods and about all the things of which I speak;
> for even if he should actually manage to say what is indeed the
>   case,
> nevertheless he himself does not know it; but belief is found
>   over all.   (frag. 34)

The fragment is cited by Sextus, and was plainly a favourite text among ancient sceptics. Sextus knows that there are different ways of construing the last couplet; and the Pyrrhonian interpretation has not been universally accepted as an accurate reading of Xenophanes. But here we are concerned with what the Pyrrhonists made of the lines, not with the correctness of their interpretation.

Sextus himself offers a nice simile or story to explain Xenophanes' meaning:

> Let us imagine that some people are looking for gold in a dark room full of treasures. It will happen that each will grasp one of the things lying in the room and think he has got hold of the gold. But none of them will be persuaded that he has hit upon the gold even if he *has* in fact hit upon it. In the same way, the crowd of philosophers has come into the world, as into a vast

14 See Jonathan Barnes, 'The Beliefs of a Pyrrhonist', *Elenchos* 4, 1983, 5–43, at pp.32–41.

house, in search of truth. But it is reasonable that the man who grasps the truth should doubt whether he has been successful. (*M* VII 52)

In the darkened treasury, someone, no doubt, will have found gold; but no one can properly claim that he has done so. In the obscure world, some philosopher, no doubt, has grasped the truth; but none can properly claim that he has done so. 'For even if he should actually manage to say what is indeed the case, nevertheless he himself does not know it.'

Sextus cites the same lines of Xenophanes again in a later context, where he offers a different and equally apt simile:

> The sceptics cleverly compare enquirers into the unclear to archers shooting at a target in the dark. It is reasonable that some will hit the target and others miss it; but it will not be known who has hit and who missed. Similarly, the truth is hidden in a deep darkness. Many statements are shot at it, but which of them agree with it and which disagree cannot be known. (*M* VIII 325)

Some nocturnal archers hit the target; but none can properly claim that he has done so. Some statements about the obscure are true; but no one can properly claim that his statement is true. 'For even if he should actually manage to say what is indeed the case, nevertheless he himself does not know it.'

In neither passage does Sextus explicitly direct his similes against an externalist account of basic knowledge. (In *M* VII he is merely concerned to interpret Xenophanes; in *M* VIII he is expressly thinking of derivative knowledge, knowledge supposedly gained by proofs.) But it is plain that the similes are readily adapted to that end. Sextus might have argued in the following fashion. Suppose a Dogmatist to adhere to an externalist epistemology of the sort we may ascribe to the Stoics. Suppose him to assert that P (and to take himself to be asserting a basic belief). Then his assertion may, of course, quite well be true. Moreover, P may well be a member of the class β. But – *ex hypothesi* – he will not claim to *know* that P is a member of the class β; for he holds that he need not know that P is a member of β in order to be justified in claiming that P is true. The whole point of the externalist theory is to allow the Dogmatist to claim that P, when P is in β, *without* also claiming that P is in β. But in that case (so Sextus might have urged), he cannot properly claim to know that P. His arrow may hit the target, he may have struck gold – that is to say, his belief may be correct. But he may not *claim* to have hit the target or struck gold or grasped a truth. For, the darkness being thick, he cannot tell whether or not he has hit the target or struck gold; and, nature being obscure, he cannot tell whether or not he has hit the truth – for he cannot tell whether or not P is in β, whether or not P is in reality a basic and a natural belief.

Now at this point it may be illuminating to look again at parts of the earlier discussions of the four Agrippan modes. At the end of my account of the mode of disagreement, I had the Dogmatist suggesting that

> You may properly use a yardstick Y to decide a problem ?Q, provided that Y in fact gives the correct procedure for deciding ?Q; you do not also need to *know* that Y gives the correct procedure for ?Q.

And the sceptic answered:

> No; if you are to use Y for ?Q, you must have reason to believe that Y gives the correct procedure for ?Q.

At the end of my account of the regressive mode, the Dogmatist toyed with the thought that

> You may properly claim to know that P on the basis of an infinite sequence of reasons Σ, provided that the reasons in Σ are in fact good reasons; you do not also need to *know* that Σ is in this respect preferable to a rival sequence Σ*.

And the sceptic answered:

> No; if you are to rest P on Σ, then you must have reason to prefer Σ to Σ*.

At the end of my account of the reciprocal mode, the sophisticated Dogmatist imagined that

> You may properly claim to know that P if P is in fact a part of a coherent and true web W; you do not also need to *know* that W is better in this respect than a rival web W*.

And the sceptic answered:

> No; if you are to base P on W, then you must have good
> reasons for preferring W to W*.

And here we now have the Dogmatist holding that

> You may properly claim to know that P if P is a natural belief,
> a member of the class β; you do not also need to *know* that
> P is a member of β.

And again the sceptic answers:

> No; if you are to hold on to P, then you must have reason to
> think that P, and not some rival P*, is a member of β.

It is plain that these pairs of Dogmatic claims and sceptical retorts
are all of the same type. It is plain, too, that in each case the
Dogmatist is relying on a sort of externalist theory and that the
sceptic is pressing the inadequacy of any externalist account of
knowledge or justified belief. And in this way the status of epistemological externalism can be seen to be the deep and fundamental
issue raised by Agrippan scepticism.

It is easy to imagine that the sceptical retorts to the externalist
claims all rely on one general epistemological principle. For we
might well suppose that Sextus is here tacitly assuming that if you
know that P, you must know that you know that P; that if you are
justified in believing that P, then you must be justified in believing
that you are justified in believing that P. The sceptical retorts and
the Sextan similes might seem to amount to this: an externalist is
not entitled to hold *that he knows* that P; therefore he is not entitled
to hold that P. For the argument implicit in the similes might
appear to run as follows: since the Dogmatist does not know that P
is in β, he does not know that he knows that P. And since he does
not know that he knows that P, he does not know that P. The
second step of this argument relies on the thesis that if x knows that
P, then x knows that x knows that P.

The modern literature contains many sophisticated discussions
of the thesis that if x knows that P then x knows that x knows that
P. The thesis is known in the trade as the KK-thesis. There is an
analogous thesis for justified belief: if x is justified in believing that
P, then x is justified in believing that x is justified in believing that P.
I call this the JBJB-thesis.

What will an externalist say to this? Well, on the externalist account, x knows that P just in case because P is in β, x believes that P. Hence x will know that he knows that P just in case x knows that because P is in β he believes that P. That being so, it is plain that an externalist will have little time for the KK-thesis (or for the JBJB-thesis). For it seems perfectly clear that, in general, someone could believe in P because Q without knowing that because Q he believes in P. In other words, it could well be true that

> because Q, x believes that P,

and false that

> x believes that (because Q, x believes that P).

For it seems quite plain that I may be ignorant of the causes of my own beliefs. For this wholly general reason, and quite apart from any particular problems which the Pyrrhonist argument may raise, an externalist will want – and have good reason – to deny that if x knows that P, then x knows that x knows that P.

And in fact it is clear that the KK-thesis is false. There are perfectly ordinary cases in which, without invoking any philosophical theory at all, I can intelligibly say: 'Good Lord. I didn't realize I still knew that.' And unless such remarks are incoherent, the KK-thesis is false.

Thus if the Pyrrhonian attack on externalism, which I have derived from Sextus' two similes, depends on the KK-thesis, then the Dogmatist is able to resist it. Now some sceptical arguments do, I think, implicitly rely on the KK-thesis. Or rather, some sceptical arguments, when they are expressed informally and without logical rigour, confuse or conflate the thought that x knows P with the quite different thought that x knows that x knows P. Any argument which makes this conflation implicitly depends upon the KK-thesis; and any argument which depends on the KK-thesis is unsatisfactory.

But the Pyrrhonian argument which I presented a few pages ago does not – or at any rate, need not – trade on the KK-thesis. For the Pyrrhonian is not concerned with whether the Dogmatist *knows* that he knows that P. He is concerned with whether the Dogmatist will *claim* that P. The archer may in fact hit the target – but he may not claim to have hit it. The gold-seeker may in fact have chanced upon a nugget – but he cannot say that he has. And according to the

Pyrrhonian argument, the Dogmatist may know something – but he must keep mum about it.

The Pyrrhonian point is this. Suppose our Dogmatist continues to claim that P – that this is an apple or that honey is sweet. The claim is advanced as an 'hypothesis'. No reasons for it are given. It is offered as a putative item of basic knowledge. The Pyrrhonist wonders if the Dogmatic claim is justified. He runs through the arguments for the hypothetical mode, and then asks the Dogmatist: 'Well, do you think you're justified in claiming that P?' What reply will he get? Now the Dogmatist will actually be justified in claiming that P (on the externalist hypothesis) provided that because P is in β he believes that P. Hence if he *claims* that he is justified in believing that P, he will in effect be claiming that because P is in β he believes that P. But *ex hypothesi* he will not make this further claim. For, as I said, the whole point and purpose of his externalist invocation of basic beliefs is that he may justifiably believe that P *without* making the further claim that because P is in β he believes in P. Thus whether or not he *is* justified in claiming that P, he will not respond to the sceptic's challenge by *claiming* that he is so justified.

What happens next? The Pyrrhonist has philanthropically brought the Dogmatist's temerity to his attention (cf. *PH* III 280). How will – how should – the Dogmatist react? In particular, will he or should he continue to maintain that P? If he *does* continue to maintain that P, then he is maintaining something which he does not believe he is justified in maintaining. It is not that he confesses, under pressure from the Pyrrhonist, that he is *not* justified in believing P. It is simply that he does not believe that he *is* justified in believing P. He suspends judgement over the question whether he is justified in believing P. And the friendly Pyrrhonist has made him aware of all this. Now it is, of course, perfectly *possible* to believe P while not believing that you are justified in believing P. But is this a *rational* state of mind to be in? Can I rationally say: 'I think that honey is sweet, but I don't think I'm justified in thinking that honey is sweet'? If I make such a report, I am confessing to a curious state of mind; I am not presenting the reasonable consequence of a respectable philosophical thesis.

If this last argument is right, has the sceptic refuted the Dogmatist? Has he shown that externalism offers no escape from the

Pyrrhonian net? Not exactly. The Pyrrhonist argument, if it is sound, shows only and exactly this: if a Dogmatist is rationally to claim that P (where P is a basic belief), then he must also be entitled to claim that P is a basic belief. If our Dogmatist is to remain a foundationalist and an externalist, then he must be able to claim (1) that P, and also (2) that P is in β; but he must not offer (2) as his justification for (1).

Can a Dogmatist do this? Can he, by some ingenious intellectual twist or turn, struggle out of the Pyrrhonist net? There is a διαφωνία here: the sceptic doubts that there is any escape from the sceptical net; the Dogmatist supposes that there must be *some* way out, if only he could find it. Is the sceptic right? Or is the Dogmatist right? I do not know – μέχρι νῦν I suspend judgement on the issue.

And so I end these chapters on a sceptical note.

But this last διαφωνία is a dispute between a Dogmatist and a sceptic – it is what I earlier called a disagreement in attitude. In that case, as I argued in the first chapter, I can after all resolve the disagreement. And I must resolve it in favour of the sceptic.

And so I end these chapters on a sceptical note.

Note on the ancient authors

In the course of this book I have cited, or referred to, various dead thinkers, some of whose names are no longer familiar. The main function of this Note is to append a short sentence of information to each name. In addition, it has seemed sensible to explain the abbreviations by which I have referred to the ancient texts.

Sextus and Galen are taken separately. Then, the other authors whom I have quoted. And finally, those authors who have been mentioned but not cited.

(1) SEXTUS EMPIRICUS:
For Sextus and his works see the Introduction, pp.vii–viii and notes 3–4. The two abbreviations are:

> PH   *Outlines of Pyrrhonism*
> M   *Against the Mathematicians*

Here, and throughout this Note, I offer an English version of the full titles. For the abbreviations I have followed the normal convention of employing a Latin title. Hence the mismatch between the full and the abbreviated versions.

All translations of Sextus, and of every other ancient text, are my own. I have tried to use the latest editions of the Greek texts. For Sextus, the standard edition is the Teubner text: *PH*, edd. H. Mutschmann and J. Mau (Leipzig, 1958²); *M* VII–XI, ed. H. Mutschmann (Leipzig, 1914); *M* I–VI, ed. J. Mau (Leipzig, 1954).

(2) GALEN:
Born in Pergamum in 129 AD, much travelled, a considerable part of his career spent in Rome and in the highest circles of society. Died early in the 3rd century AD. The most successful doctor and the leading medical scientist of his day; a trained and sophisticated philosopher; a scholar and

polymath; and in addition, a voluminous author, many of whose works have survived. (See e.g. Vivian Nutton, *From Democedes to Harvey* (London, 1988), ch.1–3.) I refer to:

adv Iul	*Against Julianus*
alim fac	*Nutritive Powers*
const art med	*On the Art of Medicine*
diff puls	*Types of Pulse*
in Hipp morb acut	*Commentary on Hippocrates' On Acute Diseases*
lib prop	*My Own Books*
loc aff	*Affected Places*
meth med	*Therapeutic Method*
nat fac	*Natural Powers*
opt doct	*The Best Form of Teaching*
ord lib prop	*The Order of My Books*
PHP	*The Doctrines of Hippocrates and Plato*
sect ingred	*On the Schools, for beginners*
subf emp	*Outline of Empiricism*
syn puls	*Summary on Pulses*
Thrasyb	*Thrasybulus*
us part	*The Use of Parts*

References are by volume and page number in the edition of C.G. Kühn (Leipzig, 1821–33) – hence the 'K'. (But *subf emp* is not in Kühn, and there 'B' stands for Max Bonnet, whose edition is most conveniently found in Karl Deichgräber, *Die griechische Empirikerschule* (Berlin, 1965²).) For most of the works cited, Kühn's text is now superseded, and I have translated from the modern editions.

(3) OTHER AUTHORS CITED:

They are listed in alphabetical order. Their relative importance is not to be inferred from the number of words given to each.

ALEXANDER of Aphrodisias: 2nd/3rd century AD; the leading Peripatetic philosopher of the age; influential commentator on Aristotle.

    in APr   *Commentary on Aristotle's Prior Analytics*

AMMONIUS, son of Hermias: *c.*440–520 AD, pupil of PROCLUS, eminent Platonist of the Alexandrian school; commentator on Aristotle.

in Int	*Commentary on Aristotle's On Interpretation*
in Porph isag	*Commentary on Porphyry's Introduction*

And from Ammonius' school:

in APr   Commentary on Aristotle's Prior Analytics

AMMONIUS Saccas: 2nd/3rd century AD, teacher of Plotinus and founder of 'Neoplatonism'.

ANATOLIUS: 3rd century AD, bishop of Laodicea, versed in philosophy and mathematics.

ARISTOTLE of Stagira: 384–322 BC, the master of those who know.

> *APr*   *Prior Analytics*
> *APst* *Posterior Analytics*
> *Met*   *Metaphysics*
> *Phys* *Physics*
> *Top*   *Topics*

CAELIUS Aurelianus: 5th century AD, medical writer who translated or paraphrased SORANUS.

morb acut   On Acute Diseases

CELSUS: 1st century AD, obscure encyclopaedist; his only surviving work:

med   On Medicine

CICERO: 106–43 BC, Roman statesman, orator and philosopher, who had a penchant for Academic scepticism.

> *fin*   *On Ends*
> *leg*   *Laws*
> *Luc*   *Lucullus*

CLEOMEDES: 4th century AD (?), author of a Stoic introduction to astronomy.

disc cycl   Elementary Theory

(The work is commonly known as:

mot circ   On the Circular Motions of the Celestial Bodies)

DAVID the Invincible: 6th/7th century AD, Armenian philosopher of the school of OLYMPIODORUS.

> *in Porph isag   Commentary on Porphyry's Introduction*
> *proleg   Prolegomena to Philosophy*

Note on the ancient authors

DIOGENES LAERTIUS: 3rd century AD (?); compiler of *Lives of the Philosophers* in ten books. The *Life* of Pyrrho, in Book IX, includes a summary account of the later Pyrrhonian philosophy.

DIOGENIANUS: 2nd century AD (?), Epicurean (?) philosopher. Fragments of a work attacking CHRYSIPPUS survive.

John DOXAPATRES of Sicily: 11th century AD, monk and commentator on HERMOGENES.

ELIAS: 6th century AD, Platonist philosopher, pupil of OLYMPIODORUS, commentator.

> in Porph isag   *Commentary on Porphyry's Introduction*
> proleg   *Prolegomena to Philosophy*

EPICTETUS: *c*.50–120 AD, ex-slave, Stoic philosopher; his conversations were transcribed by his follower, the historian Flavius Arrianus.

> diss   *Discourses*

EPICURUS of Samos: 341–270 BC, founder of the philosophical school which taught atomism and hedonism.

> ad Hdt   *Letter to Herodotus*

EPIPHANIUS: 4th century AD, rhetorician, commentator on HERMOGENES.

EUSEBIUS of Caesarea: *c*.260–340 AD, bishop, eminent churchman and prolific author.

> PE   *Preparation for the Gospel*

HERMOGENES of Tarsus: *c*.160–225 AD, rhetorical theorist, his works became objects of scholarly commentary.

> id   *On Style*
> stas   *Issues*

HERO of Alexandria: 1st century AD(?), mathematician and engineer.
> def   *Definitions*

LUCIAN of Samosata: 2nd century AD, cultivated author of numerous satirical sketches and essays.

Note on the ancient authors

MARCELLINUS: 5th/6th century AD (?), rhetorician, commentator on HERMOGENES.

NEMESIUS of Emesa: 4th/5th century AD, Christian bishop and Platonist philosopher.

  nat hom   On the Nature of Man

OLYMPIODORUS of Alexandria: 6th century AD, Platonist philosopher, pupil of AMMONIUS, commentator on Plato and Aristotle.

  in Cat   Commentary on Aristotle's Categories

PHILODEMUS of Gadara: 1st century BC, Epicurean philosopher, many of whose works are preserved on the Herculaneum papyri.

  rhet   Rhetoric

John PHILOPONUS: *c.*490–570 AD, Christian Platonist, pupil of AMMONIUS, theologian and philosopher.

  in APr   Commentary on Aristotle's Prior Analytics

Maximus PLANUDES: *c.*1225–1305, eminent Byzantine scholar and teacher, voluminous author.

PLATO of Athens: 427–347 BC, author of the dialogues to which western philosophy is a sequence of footnotes.

PORPHYRY of Tyre: 233–305 AD, pupil and biographer of Plotinus, leading Platonist philosopher.

  isag   Introduction to Philosophy

PROCLUS: *c.*410–485 AD, eminent Platonist philosopher with literary and scientific interests.

  in Eucl   Commentary on the First Book of Euclid's Elements

L. Annaeus SENECA: 4–65 AD, statesman, bellettrist and Stoic philosopher.

  apocol   Apocolocyntosis

SOPATER of Athens: 4th century AD, rhetorician, commentator on HERMOGENES.

Julius SORANUS of Ephesus: 1st/2nd century AD, leading doctor of the Methodic school.

gyn   Gynaecology

XENOPHANES of Colophon: *c*.580–480 BC, peripatetic poet and hedge-philosopher. Only fragments of his work survive.

(4) OTHER AUTHORS MENTIONED:

AENESIDEMUS of Aegae: early 1st century BC; the second founder of Pyrrhonian scepticism.

AGRIPPA: end of 1st century BC (?), Pyrrhonist. (See pp.viii–ix and 121–2.)

AMPHINOMUS: 4th century BC, mathematician.

APELLAS: 1st century BC/AD, Pyrrhonist. (See p.viii n.5)

ASCLEPIADES of Bithynia: 1st century BC, doctor and medical theorist.

CHRYSIPPUS of Soloi: *c*.280–207 BC, third head of the Stoic school and its most influential figure.

EUCLID of Alexandria: 4th/3rd century BC, leading mathematician and author of *Elements*.

FAVORINUS of Arles: 1st/2nd century AD, colourful scholar and writer, with an interest in Academic scepticism.

HIPPOCRATES of Cos: 5th century BC, doyen of Greek doctors and medical writer.

JULIANUS: 2nd century AD, Methodic doctor attacked by GALEN.

NUMENIUS of Apamea: 2nd century AD, Platonist philosopher.

PYRRHO of Elis: *c*.360–270 BC, founder and eponym of Pyrrhonian scepticism.

ZENO of Elea: 5th century BC, inventor of celebrated paradoxes.

Index of passages

The index catalogues those ancient texts which are quoted or paraphrased or commented upon. Bare footnote references are not listed.

Index of passages

Index of persons

Index of Greek terms

Index of Greek terms

Index of subjects

Index of subjects

'Internalism' (see: 'Externalism')

Justification
)(acquisition 75–6
analysed 76–7, 79–81
and disagreement 21–2, 23–4, 31–2,
   114–15
'external' 32–4, 129–30, 131, 137
and hypothesis 105–6, 108–9, 111,
   126–7
and KK-thesis 141–2
objective)(subjective 79–80
and reciprocity 59, 83–7
and regression 40, 48
(see also: Infinite regression, Proof,
   Rationality)

Knowledge
claims to 143–4
direct)(indirect 117, 121–2, 123–4,
   125, 128–30
KK-thesis 138–9, 141–3

'Links with the world' 56–7, 88–9
Logic viii, 4, 33, 38, 58–9, 59–60,
   70–2, 76, 90, 92, 106–7, 110

Magna Moralia 13–14, 21–2, 31,
   34–5, 75
Medicine 96, 99, 133
disagreements in 1–2, 2n2, 2n3, 4–6
sects of 2, 5–6, 8
and scepticism 7, 9
(see also: Asclepiades, Galen)
Metaphors 78, 82
military 7, 12–13, 12n16, 30
Method, philosophical 3–4
Methodic doctors 2n3, 7
Modes of suspension 16–17
of Aenesidemus 40–1
of Agrippa 16–17, 23, 25–6, 39, 59,
   96, 99, 113, 117n3
systems of (Chapter 5 passim), 26,
   28, 32, 42–3, 66, 98–9, 108–9
   Five Modes 114
   Four Modes 114–16
   Three Modes 119–20
   'Two' Modes 116–19, 117n3
sources for 65, 72, 100, 114, 114n2,
   117n3, 120–2
(see also: Disagreement,
   Hypothetical mode, Infinite
   regression, Reciprocity)
Motion, paradox of 45

Nature
and belief 132–7
and causation 6, 136–7
and criteria 132–3
hidden 5–6, 140
in Pyrrhonism 137–8

Obscurum per obscurius 74
Opposites 100, 101, 105–6, 127, 128,
   130

Pangolins 9
Parity of reason 54–5, 87–9, 105–6
Perception 4, 17–18, 27, 30, 41, 74,
   117, 133, 134, 137
Peripatetics 2, 3n6, 121–3
(see also: Aristotle)
Phenomena 5–6, 12, 26, 40–1, 110–11,
   137–8
(see also: Unclear)
Philosophy viii, 96, 138–9
sects in 2–3, 11–12, 30–1
Physics viii, 39n1, 117
Pores 59, 128–9, 128n10
Postulate 94, 95, 102, 106
(see also: Hypothesis)
Priority 64, 74–82
epistemic 45–6, 47, 48, 76–82,
   83–4, 85–7, 111
   asymmetrical? 77–9, 81–2, 84, 85
   defined 79–81
   transitive? 77–9, 81–2, 84, 85
temporal 74–6, 82
terminology for 74n12

Probability 22, 80
Proof 39, 40, 41, 71–3, 93, 103
Aristotelian 65, 67, 73, 76–8, 78–9,
   94
)(criterion 26–7, 29, 125
and justification 75–6
as psychological event 74–5
and syllogism 38, 59–60
(see also: Infinite regression,
   Justification)
Pyrrhonism vii–ix, 10, 24, 29, 35,
   137–8
(see also: Pyrrho, Sextus)

Rationality 21, 22, 23–4, 31–2, 34–5,
   86–7, 143–4
Reasons (see: Justification, Proof,
   Rationality)
Reciprocity (Chapter 3 passim)